D0771369

An Investors Press Guide for 401(k) Administrators

Helping Employees Achieve Retirement Security

Features Answers to the Most Often Asked 401(k) Questions

Copyright © 1995 Investors Press, Inc. Washington Depot, CT 06794.

World rights reserved. No part of this publication may be stored in a retrieval system, transmitted or reproduced in any way, including but not limited to photocopy, photograph, magnetic or other record, without the prior agreement and written permission of the Publisher. Making more than one (1) copy, and for other than strictly personal use, is absolutely prohibited. Bulk copies of this publication may be obtained as explained on the order page at the back of the book.

Copyright © 1995 by Investors Press, Inc.

All rights reserved under International and Pan-American Copyright Conventions.

Published in the United States by Investors Press.

Library of Congress Cataloging-in-Publication Data
    Investors Press
    I. Helping Employees Achieve Retirement Security
        ISBN 1-885123-04-3
           I. Helping Employees Achieve Retirement Security
Printed in Mexico

10 9 8 7 6 5 4 3 2 1

Jacket art © 1995 by Wendell Minor
Book and jacket design by Silver Communications Inc., NYC.

ACKNOWLEDGEMENT

Investors Press is pleased to publish **Helping Employees Achieve Retirement Security**, the first of two 1995 Guides for 401(k) Plan Administrators.

Each of these two original books examines issues of compelling concern to those responsible for managing and administering their organization's 401(k) plans. Written by acknowledged industry experts, each book in the Series is an easy-to-use, practical guide and an informative, continuing reference resource.

This first Guide in the Series is underwritten by a distinguished group of providers from across the country to whom special appreciation goes from everyone who values the importance of education and the candid exchange of information. Their commitment makes this book available to you—the men and women who are charged with meeting the increasingly complex daily challenges of helping your employees achieve retirement security.

INVESTORS
PRESS

Helping Employees Achieve Retirement Security
An Investors Press Guide for 401(k) Administrators

Underwritten by

Access Research, Inc.

Aetna Investment Services, Inc.

American United Life Insurance, Co. (AUL)

CIGNA Retirement & Investment Services

Fidelity Investments®

Harris Investment Management, Inc.

Kemper

LaSalle National Trust, N.A.

MetLife

NYL Benefit Services Company

Prudential

T. Rowe Price Associates, Inc.

PREFACE

Helping Employees Achieve Retirement Security is an important new resource written for you and your counterparts at more than 14,000 companies around the country.

The purpose of this Guide is to help you help your employees use their 401(k) plan to achieve retirement security. In this complex, changing world of increasing investment choices and diverse participant needs, it is essential that you have a ready source of comprehensive, reliable information to answer the daily wave of questions rolling into your office from plan participants and eligible enrollees.

Together with Building Your Nest Egg With Your 401(k)—its Investors Press sister publication written by Lynn Brenner specifically for employee plan participants and eligible enrollees—Ted Benna's **Helping Employees Achieve Retirement Security** emphasizes why it is so important for them to save as much as they can—as soon as they can. Both books examine the major issues that all employees need to understand: they explain how each kind of investment works, how different kinds of investments can be combined to provide needed returns without participants' taking on more risk than they can live with, and how they can create an investment strategy for retirement that's easy to implement.

Ted Benna is the Founder and President of The 401(k) Association, an organization he created to give participants direct access to the political process. Informally known as the "father of the 401(k)," he has been a long-time and influential benefit consultant.

Lynn Brenner, distinguished author and personal finance columnist for Newsday, a Times Mirror newspaper with more than a million readers, has been widely published in numerous respected national journals and magazines. As Contributing Editor for this Guide, she has provided invaluable information, experience and expertise.

Helping Employees Achieve Retirement Security continues our commitment to provide thoroughly researched, independent information that helps you manage and administer 401(k) plans.

INVESTORS
PRESS

Washington Depot, Connecticut

TABLE OF CONTENTS

INTRODUCTION

Y ou may be surprised to learn that although 401(k) plans are now the primary retirement savings vehicle for more than 20 million Americans, they are actually the result of a political fluke. Unlike ERISA, no aspiring or seasoned politician introduced the innovative 401(k) plan. Neither party claims it as a vital part of their political platform and 401(k)s are not championed by anyone in our government.

Without these powerful supporters, the magnitude of the tax-deferred savings enjoyed by plan participants makes the 401(k) an extremely vulnerable target for revenue-hungry politicians who discount the potential burden of supporting the growing number of employees who may not be able to provide for themselves in their retirement years.

We must all be concerned that another political fluke may make these plans disappear as quickly as they came into being.

To understand the actual evolution of 401(k) plans and their uncertain future, you need to know just one simple fact: Section 401(k) was added to the Internal Revenue Code simply to resolve a conflict between Congress and the Treasury Department over the tax-deferred profit-sharing plans many larger banks adopted to replace cash bonus plans. Participants of these profit-sharing plans could elect to receive half the amount their employers contributed as cash, or they could defer this amount into the plan for retirement or other purposes. The other half was automatically contributed to their retirement plan.

At that time, most higher-paid employees deferred the entire amount to their retirement plans to avoid the up to 50% tax consequences. Most lower-paid employees took the 50% elective amount as cash to buy Christmas presents or use for some other immediate purpose.

A New Era in Tax-Deferred Savings

As an increasing number of employees participated in this flexible profit-sharing arrangement, government officials responded with a campaign to restrict its growth. Although the cash distributions were elective, these plans appeared to provide an undesirable tax advantage to higher-paid employees, and subsequently a black cloud settled over their future. Cash and tax-deferred plans were entangled in Treasury Department and Congressional bureaucracies until Congress included a provision in ERISA that froze their tax status through 1976. This moratorium gave government officials more time to decide the future of these plans. When Congress passed the Revenue Act of 1978, Section 401(k) slid almost unnoticed into the Internal Revenue Code and unwittingly paved the way for a new era in employee tax-deferred savings.

What did Section 401(k) actually state and what did its seemingly innocuous enactment signal for tax-deferred plans? Section 401(k) added just one paragraph to the Internal Revenue Code: it required cash-deferred arrangements to meet a special non-discrimination test. Its enactment did not begin a mad rush to establish 401(k) savings plans as we know them today; most employee benefit professionals simply acknowledged that Section 401(k) made it possible for them to establish new cash-deferred profit sharing plans.

How did a few words in the Internal Revenue Code lead to a savings vehicle that now represents more than $500 billion in employee savings[1] and is an important tool that Americans use to plan and save for a safer and more secure retirement?

Fifteen years ago as I read Section 401(k) very carefully, its real value became clear to me through prayer, and I concluded that whatever was not prohibited in the Code was indeed possible.

As an owner of the Johnson Companies, an employee benefit consulting firm in Pennsylvania, I was working with a bank client who wanted to revamp its defined benefit plan and eliminate a long-standing cash bonus plan that had lost its appeal among participants. I was aware of prevailing competitive issues: most other banks offered both a defined benefit and a defined contribution plan for their employees.

I knew that Section 401(k) would enable the bank to replace its cash bonus plan with a cash or deferred profit-sharing plan. The only catch was that the plan could meet the required discrimination tests only if many of the lower-paid employees chose to participate. It seemed a safe assumption that most lower-paid employees would take cash rather than tie up their money for the sake of saving a few tax dollars. As I searched for a solution, a new idea emerged: why not have the bank contribute a $.25 or $.50 per dollar matching contribution as an incentive for plan participation?

Using the idea of a combined incentive of tax savings and matching contributions from the bank, an attractive new plan was created that would be difficult for bank employees at any income level to refuse. We used the following illustration to introduce the concept to our client:

---

[1] This is the current Access Research, Inc. estimate of total employee savings in 401(k) plans. See chart on page 12.

Elective bank contribution to the plan	$1,000.00[2]
Tax savings through the tax-deferred contribution (assuming 20% tax rate)	200.00
Employer matching contribution (at $.25 per dollar)	250.00
Dollar incentive to participate	$450.00

Creating the matching contribution was the first step in tax-deferred savings innovation. The next step was to structure a plan that would allow employees to put money into the plan each pay period through a painless automatic salary reduction.

When I presented the 401(k) concept to my board, they recommended selling the idea. We offered it to two of the country's largest insurance companies; both turned down the opportunity to take the idea to market as their own. We then decided to market the 401(k) concept ourselves.

The initial challenge was to find a "guinea pig" who would establish the first 401(k) plan. Our bank client declined because it did not want to risk implementing a new benefit program that lacked a track record. To start the ball rolling, our own company became the guinea pig: On January 1, 1981 the Johnson Companies converted their after-tax savings plan to the first 401(k) savings plan in the country.

THE REACTION FROM WASHINGTON

Ronald Reagan had just been elected with a mandate to overhaul the economy. One of his major policy objectives was to increase savings and create capital to fund economic expansion. His administration's legislative initiative was to increase personal savings through more IRA investments.

Early in 1981 I met with Congressman Jack Kemp who was spearheading President Reagan's initiative to expand IRAs. I pointed out that it wasn't necessary to expand IRAs because Section 401(k) was already on the books and would lead to even greater savings. Kemp was warned that 401(k) plans would cause the loss of $4 to $5 billion in annual tax revenue within a couple of years, a warning he ignored in his budget projections. The Reagan team proceeded with their agenda to expand IRAs and we proceeded to market 401(k) plans.

More than $10 billion of tax revenue losses each year through 1994 outpaced even my predictions; now the politicians are really paying attention.

HUMBLE BEGINNINGS

Marketing the 401(k) concept was difficult; attracting media interest was even harder. The first article appeared in *The Philadelphia Inquirer* and the reporter got hundreds of calls from employee benefit and tax professionals who proclaimed that what I was trying to do was illegal. There was a general skepticism, as well, that lower-paid workers would not participate.

The 401(k) gained national attention with a subsequent *New York Times* article. Momentum started to build. Large companies began to convert existing thrift

---

[2] The bank has specified $1,000 as their contribution. The employee can take the $1,000 as a cash bonus or defer it into the 401(k) plan to avoid paying current taxes.

plans or establish new 401(k) savings plans in early 1981. The next wave of 401(k) plans was established that year when the Treasury Department issued regulations supporting the concept. By the time the Reagan team started their tax reform process, many of the country's largest employers had already initiated 401(k) plans.

A CAMPAIGN TO ELIMINATE 401(k) PLANS

The Reagan policy team rationalized that, despite the enormous good 401(k)s provided by helping Americans plan and save for retirement, the resulting tax losses warranted a campaign to eliminate them. It seemed incomprehensible to me that a President who had been elected a few years earlier on a personal savings platform could propose killing a program that fulfilled his own campaign promise.

But the Reagan administration's efforts to kill 401(k) plans actually rallied the participant troops. Thousands of 401(k) participants, eager to protect and defend their plans, wrote to their Congressmen demanding action to prevent the assassination of the 401(k). One senator's staff started counting the number of bags of mail from participants, rather than the number of letters.

A ground swell of participant activism was no match for President Reagan's effort to generate more immediate annual tax revenue. The government modified the Tax Reform Act of 1986 (TRA), drastically reducing the maximum amount employees could contribute to 401(k) plans each year from $30,000 to $7,000, and imposing more restrictive and complex non-discrimination tests.

THE DANGER REMAINS

The survival of 401(k)s is still threatened. Some policymakers view them as the evil usurper of defined benefit plans. Although there is no doubt that the tax revenue lost to 401(k) plans could indeed help to reduce the deficit or fund new programs, Washington continues to undervalue their long-term social and economic benefits.

My belief that the future of 401(k)s remains fragile and tenuous led to my founding The 401(k) Association in 1993 as a voice and resource for plan participants. Although another direct attack like the one during the Reagan tax reform days is unlikely, an indirect tax increase—such as reducing further the amount of money employees may contribute to a 401(k) or an IRA—could be deadly.

SOCIAL POLICY VERSUS FISCAL RESPONSIBILITY

After the Tax Reform Act of 1986, 401(k)s enjoyed a legislative reprieve until the passage of the Unemployment Compensation Act of 1992, a political initiative that had little if any direct correlation to 401(k)s. This is a classic example of the continuing conflict that threatens the security of 401(k)s: social policy versus fiscal responsibility. Politicians struggle to fund unemployment benefit extensions through spending reductions or by raising revenue. The benefit extension passed with the Unemployment Compensation Act was funded by imposing tax withholding on distributions from retirement plans such as 401(k)s. This caused costly plan compliance issues and administrative nightmares.

The Clinton tax bill of 1993 imposed a $150,000 compensation limit on all qualified retirement plans, and thereby reduced the amount of lost tax revenue from the highest-paid employees. Because this new compensation limit also applies to the special non-discrimination tests these plans must satisfy, many participants earning over $66,000 had to reduce their contributions and suffer an indirect tax increase. Unfortunately, some employers terminated their 401(k) plans in response to the maximum compensation limit, resulting in the loss of this tax-favored benefit for both their higher-paid and lower-paid employees.

The 1994 GATT trade bill is another example of how vulnerable 401(k) plans are to seemingly unrelated legislation. In an effort to generate revenue that would offset tax losses, the GATT bill changed the way maximum 401(k) contributions are calculated, allowing only incremental, periodic increases until further legislation is passed.

THE CURRENT THREAT TO 401(k)S

Another major, unresolved threat to 401(k)s is the Uniformed Services Employment and Reemployment Act of 1994. It intends to restore lost benefits to men and women called to active duty during Desert Storm; confusion remains about its effective date and whether it covers any prior military service.

What employer is likely to have the records necessary to determine the benefits lost during any military conflict since 1940? Compliance will be difficult, if not impossible. There is enormous liability exposure from current and former employees; plan sponsors will be forced to evaluate whether the burden of potential liabilities outweighs the benefits to current 401(k) participants.

THE FUTURE FOR 401(k)S

The fact that 401(k)s are a relatively easy tax revenue target does not seem to diminish their popularity. The number of these plans increases each year. There will be even more of them if pressure grows for government to replace their 457 plans with more flexible 401(k) plans.

Recent data from Access Research, Inc., a specialist in defined contribution plan research, indicates that 401(k) assets doubled over the past five years and projects that they will double again in the next five years. What's behind this extraordinary growth?

- ➤ Increasing participation rates in current plans
- ➤ Continued rapid new plan formation (especially among small and mid-size firms)
- ➤ Wage increases
- ➤ 77 million Baby Boomers (one-third of the country's total population) expanding the pre-retirement age group
- ➤ Increasing awareness of the need to save for retirement
- ➤ The continuing switch from traditional defined benefit to defined contribution plans

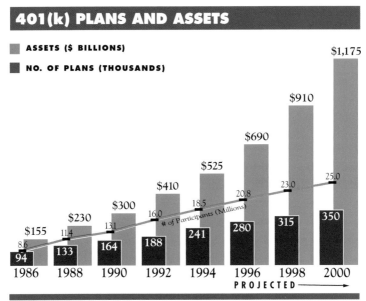

401(k) PLANS AND ASSETS

■ ASSETS ($ BILLIONS)

■ NO. OF PLANS (THOUSANDS)

$1,175

$910

$690

$525

$410

$300

$230

$155

# of Participants (Millions)

	1986	1988	1990	1992	1994	1996	1998	2000
Participants	8.6	11.4	13.1	16.0	18.5	20.8	23.0	25.0
No. of Plans	94	133	164	188	241	280	315	350

PROJECTED ──────▶

SOURCE: ACCESS RESEARCH, INC.

In anticipation of the 25th anniversary of the first 401(k) plan, here are a dozen predictions for January 1, 2006:

1. The number of 401(k) plans will have tripled, and assets will have climbed to $2 trillion.

2. The Social Security normal retirement age will have increased from 67 to 70.

3. Social Security benefits will be fully taxable for many recipients.

4. Twenty-first century work force entrants will not receive benefits from the present Social Security system.

5. All compensation will be subject to the full FICA tax.

6. The number of private sector defined benefit qualified plans among employers with more than 500 employees will have decreased by at least 50%.

7. Participants who move from one employer's 401(k) plan to another's will be eligible *immediately* to join the new employer's plan.

8. Lump sum cash payouts will be legislated out of existence. Participants will be required to leave their money in a 401(k) plan or transfer it directly into a rollover IRA and take periodic distributions.

9. Legislation will be passed to establish mandatory participant investment guidelines, full expense disclosure to participants and specific investor education requirements.

10. Participants will select from a huge variety of funds. Pre-packaged allocation mixes will continue to be available in new forms for those who do not wish to make investment allocation decisions.

11. More and more often, participants will hire an investment professional to make their 401(k) investment decisions.

12. Finally, there will be massive industry consolidation. Most plans will be administered by a few major service providers who continue to sustain major investments in new and improved technology.

PROTECTING 401(k)s: EDUCATION IS THE BEST DEFENSE

As we look to the future, we must remember that no other available retirement plan gives individuals such freedom to choose and control their own investments and to influence their retirement outcome.

Although many factors influence each participant's ability to reach his or her retirement objectives, none is so powerful as the legislator's hand. Plan sponsors and participants alike must acknowledge that their 401(k) plans will not continue exactly as they know them today. Not only do participants need to be educated about the process of saving and investing, they need to be schooled in the workings of Washington. Employers and employees must watch pending legislative actions carefully and write immediately to their Congressmen whenever one dollar of their nest egg appears to be in financial jeopardy.

The best defense against threats to the survival of 401(k) plans is participant education. The more your participants know, and the more skilled they become as savers and long-term investors, the less likely it is that legislators will be able to find some "invisible" way to eliminate or reduce the benefits of these valuable plans.

This 401(k) Administrator's Guide will educate, inform and empower you as you help your participants prepare for a secure retirement. With an increased understanding of 401(k)s and clear, concise answers to the most commonly asked participant questions, plan administrators and participants together can become a powerful force—too strong for Washington to ignore.

R. Theodore Benna

CHAPTER
ONE

DAILY VALUATION: TO SWITCH OR NOT TO SWITCH?

F inding the best valuation frequency for 401(k) plans continues to be a perplexing task for many administrators. The debate centers on concern that daily valuations—and the ability to make more frequent or possibly daily investment transfers—will convert participants from long-term investors into market timers. Since participants are usually criticized for parking their 401(k) money in the most conservative funds, the question is: does daily valuation transform these seemingly risk-averse savers into market timers simply because they can transfer money in their accounts more frequently?

In fact, many 401(k) plan sponsors and providers believe that participants who can make daily investment transfers actually feel *less* urgency to change their investment allocations. Participants who can make investment transfers *only* at the beginning of each month or each quarter may actually have a stronger motivation to "act now" rather than wait.

In 1993, Firstar of Milwaukee[1] changed to daily valuations, enabling participants to make investment transfers through a voice response system. According to Tom Hatcher, some participants enter an investment transfer on the voice response system and then hang up before they confirm the transaction. "Apparently, knowing they can make the change at any time stops some participants from doing so," explained Hatcher, when he was First Vice President with Firstar.

IBM's[2] experience with participant transfers is similar to Firstar's: requests occur on average every 2.5 years *per participant* and this data supports their probable move to daily valuation, according to Art Amler, Project Manager for Capital Accumulation Programs in IBM's U.S. human resource organization, Workforce Solutions.

---

[1] Firstar of Milwaukee is a Wisconsin-based bank with total 401(k) plan assets of $272 million and 9,170 participants representing 89% of eligible employees.
[2] IBM has total 401(k) plan assets of approximately $7 billion and 180,000 participants; 90% of eligible employees are in the plan.

Marvin Damsma, Director of Trust Investments at Amoco[3], supports daily valu-ations, emphasizing that their 35,000 participants should not have to make investment decisions at the same time. He acknowledges that the potential exists for participants to compete for "trader of the month," but Amoco has not experi-enced this phenomenon. Damsma also raises a logical point: "If you're a long-term investor, why do you read the Wall Street Journal every day?" Investors may not change their portfolios after reading the daily investment news, but it is certainly their prerogative.

Tracking trading activity for the 900,000 participants it services, one leading mutual fund provider indicates that during 1993 only about 50% of their partici-pants contacted their service center:

PARTICIPANT ACTIVITY	PERCENTAGE OF GROUP
No contact	50%
Requested information but did not make a change	37%
Made one investment change	8%
Made two or more investment changes	5%

Apple Computer's[4] experience supports these findings. Benefits Manager Sally Gottlieb notes that "We used to have quarterly valuations and changed to daily. Many people think the number of transactions goes up with that kind of switch; we found the opposite is true." Apple's participants call often for information but very few make actual transactions.

Not all plan sponsors agree, however. Kathy Guthormsen, Risk Manager of Autodesk, Inc.[5], believes that their plan's switch to daily valuations has led to its participants' obsession with short-term performance. "This was demonstrated clearly during a recent market decline. The employee benefits people had to fight to get participants to think long-haul."

But even if daily valuations don't turn participants into market timers, this system is not the best fit for every plan. When plan sponsors select investment managers to manage a portfolio of individual securities instead of using off-the-shelf funds, it may not be feasible for these portfolios to be valued daily. Inge Pihl Spungen, Director of Finance at Cravath, Swaine & Moore, says her management team rates investment performance higher than frequent valuation cycles. "We're not about to disrupt our investment program to make the switch to daily valua-tions," she explains.

If you are concerned that daily valuations will turn your participants into active traders, a simple solution is to continue to limit the number of times they

---

[3] Amoco, the Chicago-based oil conglomerate, has total 401(k) plan assets of $2.8 billion and 35,000 participants.
[4] Apple Computer, based in Cupertino, CA, has total 401(k) plan assets of $160 million and 8,000 participants representing 87% of eligible employees.
[5] Autodesk is a San Rafael, CA-based manufacturer of design and multimedia software with total 401(k) plan assets of $21 million and 1,400 participants representing 85% of eligible employees.

can change investments. But keep your decision to switch to daily valuations in a realistic context: *your participants' retirement goals will not be met simply because you change the number of times they can make investment transfers.*

What are the advantages of changing to daily valuations? These seven benefits often convince plan sponsors to make the switch:

1. **Access to current account balance information**. It is frustrating for participants to have ready access to information about their bank account balances—but limited access to information about their typically larger 401(k) accounts.

2. **Convenience**. Participants enjoy the freedom to change investment options when they wish, rather than only on pre-determined days each year.

3. **Speed**. The cutting-edge technology of the daily valuation system speeds up plan administrative procedures.

4. **Accuracy**. Participant account records are maintained automatically on a real-time basis with investment income credited from the date invested to the date withdrawn.

5. **Benefit payments include investment income and loss up to the time the check is processed**. This eliminates the need to explain why interest isn't paid during the gap period between the last valuation and the payment date—a frequent source of confusion as account balances grow.

6. **Participants do not absorb investment losses as a result of other participant terminations**. This is a major benefit when substantial distributions are triggered by events such as divestitures and staff reductions.

7. **The competitive factor**. Daily valuations attract and retain potential employees who have experienced the benefits and convenience of this state-of-the-art system at other companies.

Saving Time Means Saving Money

Most plan sponsors leave no stone unturned as they search for ways to reduce costs. It is a misconception that daily valuation systems are more expensive than their monthly or quarterly counterparts. In fact, daily valuations typically cost about the same as monthly valuations, and only about 10% more than quarterly valuations. Plan administrators can also reap substantial savings when the daily valuation system automation reduces internal staff.

For many, the time-worn adage that "time is money" is a perfect argument for switching to a daily valuation system. An investment transfer, for example, is generated electronically and captured within the recordkeeping system. Each transfer occurs after a simple telephone call from the participant. There isn't any paper to process, and participants feel they are receiving better service with little or no added cost to the plan.

In contrast is the laborious, multi-step process of making an investment transfer within a "traditional" recordkeeping system:

1. Participant obtains the transfer form.

2. Participant completes and returns the form to the 401(k) administrator.

3. The administrator advises the recordkeeper that the transfer has been requested by sending a copy of the form.

4. The recordkeeper manually enters the transfer into the system.

5. The system computes the amount that is to be transferred during the valuation cycle.

6. The administrator receives a report showing the amount to be transferred from one fund to another.

7. The administrator sends the investment manager written instructions to transfer the appropriate amount of money.

One simple transaction requires seven time-consuming steps, and invites the human errors that result from labor-intensive recordkeeping.

Good Payroll Data: A Daily Valuation Prerequisite

The quality and accessibility of your payroll data is an important factor to consider: a daily valuation system is not for plan sponsors who have difficulty providing accurate payroll data to their recordkeepers.

Each participant's account stands alone within a daily valuation system, much like a personal bank or mutual fund account. Transactions are entered independently into each participant's account, and the account builds transaction by transaction. Activity in the account of one participant does not impact any other participant's account. Each account is updated for contributions, dividends, investment transfers, and so on, every day. An inaccurate payroll tape is a serious problem because each error must be corrected manually in the system, and all subsequent transactions must be examined to determine if an adjustment is necessary.

Conversely, with a traditional valuation system, participant accounts are processed in the aggregate after transactions occur. For example, the primary objective of a quarterly valuation is to balance the books so that participant account balances match total plan assets. Investment return, for example, is credited to all participant accounts at the end of the valuation period, rather than each time there is a dividend or capital gain distribution. There is ample time to adjust entries or to correct an error from a prior valuation period. An adjustment that affects all participants can be accomplished by merely increasing or decreasing the investment gain or loss to be allocated among the participant accounts. Correcting data problems is not easy with a traditional valuation system, but it is not as daunting as it is with daily valuations.

Sequa Corporation[6] recently changed recordkeepers—a time when many plan sponsors consider moving to daily valuations. According to Jack Krupinsky, Compensation Manager, payroll handling was a major factor in Sequa's decision to move from quarterly to only monthly valuations. Sequa's payroll processing is decentralized; this makes it difficult to get the timely, accurate data needed for daily valuations.

SERVICE PROVIDERS: FUELING THE DAILY VALUATION DEBATE

The daily versus non-daily valuation debate continues with hardly a nod to industry-changing trends at the service provider level. Most recordkeepers currently use one of about half a dozen major systems. The future of the business is in the hands of companies who have invested heavily in the development of daily valuation systems and who bear the financial burden of the major updating required as new laws and regulations are passed.

Recordkeeping organizations have made major investments in daily valuation systems and in hiring or retraining personnel. Many now operate both traditional and daily valuation systems, but they are unlikely to continue to incur the double expense of two independent recordkeeping systems that require separate software maintenance fees, hardware systems and maintenance fees, computer technicians and operating personnel.

Your recordkeeper may soon tell you that you have no choice but to convert to their new system. You may not be able to maintain your current valuation cycle. Some service providers will ask you to change to daily valuations or find another provider. If you must go through the hassle of a system conversion, it makes sense to change to daily valuations and take advantage of the benefits the new system offers.

MAKING THE MOVE TO DAILY VALUATIONS: MORE THAN MEETS THE EYE

Converting from traditional to daily valuations requires a complete system conversion with the same headaches involved in changing recordkeepers—even if you stay with the same service provider. One of the most challenging issues is the "blackout period": while you convert to a daily valuation system, all plan activity is suspended. All participant accounts must be converted into the number of fund shares or units as of the day the daily valuation system begins operations. Some

---

[6] Sequa Corporation is a New York-based conglomerate with total 401(k) plan assets of $80 million and 4,300 participants representing 79% of eligible employees.

recordkeepers require the conversion of all assets to cash during the black-out period. Others permit participants to move their money into the new investment funds prior to the conversion so that the funds remain invested as the participants directed during the conversion process.

If a plan undergoes the major change to daily valuations, it makes sense to expand the number and type of investment options and add other services—a voice response system, for example. Explaining these changes and new services to participants is the next major challenge.

SMART PILLS

➤ If you are concerned about your participants turning into market timers, consider limiting the number of times investment transfers can be made.

➤ Do not consider daily valuations if you have significant payroll data problems that make it difficult for you to provide your recordkeepers with accurate, timely information.

➤ Recognize that changing to daily valuations is a complicated move—it requires careful planning and extensive explanation to participants.

➤ Consider acting before you are acted on: whatever your opinion is on daily valuation systems, recognize that in the very near future service providers may force you to make the switch.

Special
Delivery

A retirement package you can feel good about.

A retirement package you can feel good about is one that fits your business needs. What makes our package special? It's not just the standard services you expect from a retirement program. It's a team that works with you to design the right plan and is dedicated to helping you and your employees make informed retirement decisions. Personal service and retirement expertise – we've got everything you need to feel good about your retirement package. To learn more about our services, call Edward J. Lavelle, Senior Vice President, Aetna Investment Services, Inc. at (203) 273-5866.

Employee Communication:
What Should Plan Administrators Provide?

W hat should you tell your employees about their 401(k) plan? Plan administrators probably struggle with this question more than any other.
Communicating with your employees is always a challenge; it takes top
priority whether you establish a new plan, expand a young plan or maintain a
mature plan.

When plan sponsors decide how much to communicate to participants they are
usually driven by two basic motivations: self-protection and altruism. Some are
concerned primarily with minimizing their liability exposure. They do what the
law requires—no more, no less. Others see communication as a way of helping
employees meet their retirement needs and recognize that making participants less
dependent on the company as they make more and more investment decisions on
their own is a good business strategy.

Although compliance with the Department of Labor's 404(c) voluntary regulations requires employers to provide participants with enough information to make
informed investment decisions, the definition of "enough information" invites
varying definitions and creates confusion for many plan sponsors about what is
required for compliance.[7]

Furthermore, communication policies are often influenced by plan administrators' professional advisors. Advocates of the minimal approach believe participants
might attribute investment losses or funding shortfalls to misleading or flawed
information provided by the plan sponsor. These advisors warn that the more
information provided, the more room for error and the greater the risk of future
liability for the sponsor.

Advisors at the other extreme believe that participants who accumulate inadequate nest eggs will blame plan sponsors for not providing enough information
about how much money they actually needed. It's difficult to dismiss this concern,

---

[7] For an extensive discussion of 404(c) regulations among 401(k) plan administrators and legal
experts, see **A Wing and A Prayer: Defined Contribution Plans and the Pursuit of 24
Karat Golden Years**, pp. 69-79, Investors Press, 1994.

even when it comes from parties with vested interests—independent education consultants, or providers who promote their 401(k) services by distributing free educational materials.

This damned-if-we-do, damned-if-we-don't dilemma makes it difficult for plan sponsors to decide how much to educate participants through various forms of communication. Nonetheless, all 401(k) plan sponsors share the same goal: attaining and sustaining an adequate level of plan participation.

Many 401(k) communication efforts focus on selling the participants plan *features*, such as reduced taxes or matching contributions, rather than emphasizing *how to invest* to achieve an adequate nest egg. This leads to increasing concern among benefit professionals that too many participants may not accumulate enough money for retirement. Plan representatives must create and maintain education programs that help participants become better retirement savers, planners and long-term investors.

Today's approximately 20 million 401(k) participants have diverse information needs. Within your own company there are eligible employees who haven't joined the plan, and others who are ready to retire with hefty account balances. How can you meet the individual needs of such a wide range of employees? Here are a few ideas, practiced with impressive results by your colleagues at plans large and small:

➤ Individual attention and family involvement have yielded excellent results in the education effort at Autodesk, Inc.[8] This company strengthens its program (e-mail updates, annual meetings featuring investment providers, and investment skills instruction) with one-on-one financial planning sessions for participants and their families conducted by an independent 401(k) education provider. Planning sessions are paid for by the company; plan participation increased by 6% as a direct result.

➤ After moving to monthly valuations and increasing its investment options from two to four funds, Formax[9] conducted seminars as part of an intensive communication program. According to David Brown, Vice President, participants' aggregate investment mix went from a 70% fixed income/30% equity ratio to a 30%/25%/25%/20% mix on a scale of conservative to aggressive fund options. The plan now has 90% participation.

Formax goes one step further than most: periodically the company's finance department runs projections to determine how much retirement income every employee can expect based on their individual contribution levels. *This information is not distributed to employees*; it is used to identify those most in need of communication and education. Why do this? Says Brown, "We want to target employees who do not appear to be saving enough for retirement so that we can approach them individually and encourage them to increase their contributions."

---

[8] Autodesk is a San Rafael, CA-based manufacturer of design and multimedia software with total 401(k) plan assets of $21 million and 1,400 participants representing 85% of eligible employees.

[9] Formax is a Mokena, IL-based manufacturer of fast-food processing equipment with total 401(k) plan assets of $8 million and 200 participants representing 90% of eligible employees.

➤ James Wong, former Retirement Plan Administrator at Micron Technologies,[10] believes you can't provide too much educational support to plan participants. Micron's multi-tiered program consists of a computer network that posts fund performance and provides daily account information; worksheets to help participants evaluate their risk profile and retirement needs; orientation meetings for new employees; and newsletters, payroll stuffers and other literature from its investment provider. In addition, Wong personally conducts quarterly seminars and question-and-answer meetings for plan participants. Except for the materials furnished by its investment provider, Micron pays for all communications.

➤ The Ryland Group,[11] hired Standard & Poor's to help participants make more informed investment decisions, according to Dan High, Director of Benefits & Compensation. An annual report features a risk analysis of each investment fund, along with six asset allocation models participants can use. The report assesses current market conditions as well as historical results. The company gets this information from an independent, recognized authority that has no financial interest in the 401(k) business.

➤ Some 60% of Dayton Progress Corporation's[12] participants use the retirement income modeling software (available on disk and at the worksite) provided by the company's investment manager. The company also distributes personal finance publications from the Financial Literacy Center. As Rosemary Domanski, Communications Specialist explains, "We don't want to tell employees where to put their money. We give them as much information as we can to help them make sound decisions and meet their objectives."

➤ Similarly, at Coors[13] "we want to make our work force as self-sufficient as possible," says Rex Gooch, Benefits Manager. "We want our employees to save enough to maintain their standard of living and enjoy their retirement. The company's image is enhanced when our retirees are living comfortably." Coors believes company involvement is the essence of retirement planning. Once employees grasp the importance of retirement planning, it's easier to help them formulate their personal strategies.

Since Coors launched this aggressive retirement planning campaign in 1990, 401(k) participation has increased from 73% to 89% and the average contribution rate has increased by 2% of compensation. GIC investments have dropped from an aggregate 90% to 74% and are still falling.[14]

---

[10] Micron Technologies is a Boise, ID-based diversified computer chip manufacturer with total 401(k) plan assets of $50 million and 4,500 participants representing 75% of eligible employees.

[11] The Ryland Group is a Bethesda, MD-based home builder with total 401(k) plan assets of $40 million and 2,500 participants.

[12] Dayton Progress Corporation, a Dayton, OH-based manufacturer, has 600 401(k) plan participants representing 85% of eligible employees.

[13] Adolph Coors Company is a Golden, CO-based brewery with total 401(k) plan assets of $299 million and 4,741 participants representing 89% of eligible employees.

[14] "Case Study: Leading Employees Through the Maze" by Rex Gooch, *Pension World*, July 1994, pp. 28-31.

➤ Baker Hughes[15] recently completed an extensive educational effort for its 401(k) plan. Its human resources staff traveled to company sites throughout the country—including offices with only 15 employees—to conduct two-hour meetings on various benefit enhancements, according to Phil Rice, Vice President of Human Resources. Before these meetings the participation rate was a respectable 85%. But the company was concerned about the other 15%, as well as with the fact that over 75% of participant assets were in fixed-income investments. "Our major objective," says Rice, "was to sound a wake-up call to let people know they may not have enough money at retirement."

➤ How does a manufacturer like Toyota[16] achieve its impressive 89% participation rate? Toyota doesn't wait for employees to reach eligibility; the company starts its 401(k) education during its new employee orientation week. According to Sheila Evans, Benefits Specialist, employees are encouraged to sign up for the plan even though they won't be eligible for six months. "On average, 75% of new employees sign up the day they hear about the plan, and usually, they do not change their minds about participation during that waiting period."

Toyota also showcases its 401(k) plan at its annual company picnic. Employees and their families watch informational videos while they chat with representatives from the plan's investment managers. Wava Farris, Manager of Benefits and Compensation, reports that "because of our educational efforts, participants really appreciate the 401(k) and are good about spreading the word among their co-workers."

TIPS TO HELP YOU AVOID LIABILITY

Communicating complex investment concepts to a diverse group of 401(k) participants is a tall order that invites potentially serious legal exposure.

Precise terminology is an important and simple line of defense. Plan sponsors and their providers should not be casual about using terms like "guaranteed" and "income." "Guaranteed," in fact, was hardly an appropriate word to apply to a GIC option if the GIC fund was with Executive Life or Mutual Benefit, the well-known insurers who failed as a result of overexposure to risky investments. Smart plan administrators have switched to safer, descriptive terms such as "principal retention" and "money market."

Never tell participants that a particular investment option is "safe." *Every investment option involves some possibility of loss*, including U.S. government securities. Tell your participants about the risk/reward relationships among the investment options you provide so they can have realistic expectations and make informed choices. Describe relative degrees of risk; don't simply state that an investment is "low risk" or "high risk." All verbal and written communications should describe clearly and accurately the circumstances that may result in a loss.

---

[15] Baker Hughes Inc. is a Houston, TX-based oil field service company with total 401(k) plan assets of $400 million and 10,000 participants representing 85% of eligible employees.

[16] Toyota's Georgetown, KY manufacturing division has total 401(k) plan assets of $74 million and 5,265 participants representing 89% of eligible employees.

Explaining the Investment Transfer Process

The timing of the investment transfer process is a continuing source of misunderstanding between plan sponsors and participants. Participant communication materials should explain, step-by-step, the time it takes to value an account—before the transfer occurs.

Plans that have quarterly valuations usually permit transfer requests—and written communications usually state that money may be transferred from one fund to another—on the first day of each quarter. Participants who request transfers on April 1 expect their money to be transferred on that date, *an impossibility because the value of accounts will not be known until after the March 31 valuation has been completed.* Delaying the transfer until the valuation is completed leaves the sponsor open to potential liability, especially when the delay and its consequences have not been explained to participants in advance.

It is dangerous to give false expectations to participants. Unexpected delays lead to lost opportunities (requests to transfer 20% of participants' money market assets into a growth fund in a rising market), or—worse still—a major loss (requests to transfer out of a growth fund just before the stock market rapidly declines).

Transfer problems are less likely to occur with daily valued plans because transfers occur on or about the date of the request. What is the best way to deal with investment transfers in a non-daily valued system? Some plan sponsors make up gains and losses resulting from delayed transfers, rather than risk facing a lawsuit; most make estimated transfers on the transfer date, and transfer the balance after the valuation is completed. Others tell participants about the delay so they can plan their investment strategy accordingly.

Voice Response Systems

Voice response systems, widely adopted by 401(k) plans, can be a communications trouble-spot. As handy as these systems may be for handling participant information and transaction requests, sponsors must exercise caution in how they represent their use.

Some plan communications tell participants they can pick up the phone and implement a transfer 24 hours a day, seven days a week. That sounds good, but is it always true? Even the best system will have periods of call overload, particularly during market scares. Participants who are locked out may be angry and disappointed that their expectations—based on company promises—were not met; even worse, they might blame any investment losses on system delays.

Lock-out is only one problem. Even when participants reach your voice response system, there still may be confusion about the timing of the transfer. Again, you must communicate clearly the fact that 24-hour, seven-day-a-week access to the system does not trigger instant investment transfers. Having a participant hang up the phone thinking the transfer has been completed when it hasn't been is dangerous.

Written and verbal communications should warn participants that they will not always have immediate access to the voice response system, and that you are not responsible for their inability to get through. Participants might still argue that the system has inadequate capacity; the sponsor must be able to demonstrate sound planning

and a history of fair warning through repeated and conspicuous disclaimers about the suspension or delay of transfer activity.

ACCOUNT BALANCE PROJECTIONS: WATCH THE SNAKE OIL!

Do you remember the radio commercials rampant in the early days of IRAs with their suggestion that if you put $2,000 a year into an IRA you, too, could become a millionaire and ride around in a chauffeur-driven limousine? Most people realized these scenarios were exaggerations. But how many people ever thought about inflation—the critical, invisible element missing from the picture?

Today, many 401(k) professionals get equally overzealous when they demonstrate the magic of compounding. The picture of potential wealth they paint is just as misleading *if they ignore* the impact inflation will have during several decades of asset accumulation.

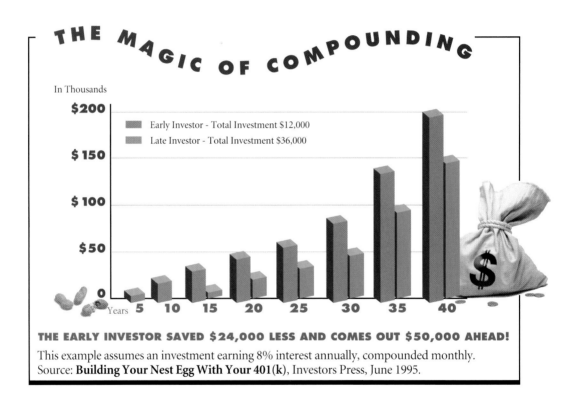

THE MAGIC OF COMPOUNDING

In Thousands

- Early Investor - Total Investment $12,000
- Late Investor - Total Investment $36,000

THE EARLY INVESTOR SAVED $24,000 LESS AND COMES OUT $50,000 AHEAD!

This example assumes an investment earning 8% interest annually, compounded monthly.
Source: **Building Your Nest Egg With Your 401(k)**, Investors Press, June 1995.

If you must use projections that are not adjusted for inflation, indicate that important fact. If your recordkeeper includes a projected account balance on participant statements—or if any service provider does so in any communications they provide—ask them to insert a conspicuous note about the impact of inflation. While this "disclaimer" does not eliminate the possibility of lawsuits, it's a wise precaution. You might also explain account projections and the effects of inflation to participants during financial and retirement planning workshops.

HOW INFLATION SHRINKS THE VALUE OF A DOLLAR

	1968	1988	% INCREASE
CORN FLAKES	24 ¢	$1.16	383%
1/2 GALLON OF MILK	45	.93	107
1 LB. BACON	69	1.79	160
McDONALDS HAMBURGER	15	.65	334

Source: Data from Statistical Abstract of the United States as it appears in **Building Your Nest Egg With Your 401(k)**, Investors Press, June 1995.

FUTURE LAWSUITS ON THE HORIZON?

If you are concerned about the possibility of future lawsuits from employees who haven't accumulated enough for retirement, you may want to discuss with your plan attorney including a statement like the following in your communication material:

> XYZ Company is pleased to sponsor this 401(k) savings plan. The purpose of the plan is *to help you save* for retirement. XYZ Company may provide information periodically to help you manage your plan account; however, XYZ Company *is not in any way responsible for the ultimate adequacy of your retirement income.*
>
> It is *your responsibility* to determine how much you should contribute and how to invest the money in your plan account to ensure that, *considering the impact of inflation*, you will still have enough money to meet your retirement needs.

THE PRICE TAG

Intense competition and the realization that plan participants, not plan sponsors, are their ultimate clients have compelled many 401(k) service providers to produce better 401(k) communications—newsletters, workbooks, retirement planning software—available free or for a modest cost. Given the growing demand for educational support, much more of these materials will come from independent organizations other than traditional defined contribution plan providers.

How to pay for educational support and information continues to be an issue. Depending on the size of your participant and eligible enrollee pool, costs can become significant. Some companies foot the whole bill. In many cases, however, the plan participants absorb all these costs; other plan sponsors share costs with the plan. Although there are rules about what expenses can be paid by the plan, generally, spending a few basis points[17] of the plan assets to fund educational efforts should be an acceptable plan expense.

Despite the cost, the need for investment education continues to grow in step with participant account balances and higher levels of participation. Plan administrators must consider a range of communications programs that satisfies both legal guidelines and altruistic goals for an increasingly diverse work force.

SMART PILLS

➤ Keep in mind the four major employee groups your communication efforts must target: non-savers, savers, novice investors and more experienced investors.

➤ Consider spending a few basis points as a plan expense to provide adequate independent educational material and investment support for your participants.

➤ The first rule of communication: consider the specific—and diverse—needs of your participants.

➤ Keep abreast of communication programs at other companies.

➤ Analyze your communication materials: are they helping to increase plan enrollment?

➤ Train employees to help educate their peers. Consider asking recent and soon-to-be retirees to share their experiences and suggestions.

➤ Launch an ongoing communication/education effort that uses a variety of resources: statement stuffers, newsletters, software programs, retirement planning workbooks, videos, cassettes, seminars.

➤ Take advantage of educational materials available from your service providers.

➤ Make sure material supplied by your service providers is objective; it should not promote one type of fund over others.

➤ Beware of wolves in sheep's clothing. Avoid using individuals or organizations who offer 401(k) services as a means to sell participants their products and services.

➤ Ask your participants for feedback about the information they receive and would like to get. *Communication must be a two-way street.*

---

[17] 100 basis points equals 1%.

MetLife Uses a Positive Educational Focus to Explain 401(k) Retirement Planning. Our Goal-Oriented, "You-Can-Do-It" Tone Is Encouraging. Our Flexible Enrollment Materials Are Thorough Yet Easy to Understand. And Our National Network of Experienced Enrollment Teams Instill a Comfort and Confidence Level That Equips Participants to Make Better Decisions. The Result? Quality Plan Enrollments.

A 401(k) Plan That's Easy for Employees to Understand

MetLife Is a Full-Service, Single-Source Provider of Custom Defined Contribution Plans. For More Information, Including Details on MetAssure™, Our Participation Guarantee, Call Gary Lineberry at 1-212-578-3181.

Educate
Communicate

MetLife
Defined Contribution Group

Metropolitan Life Insurance Company
One Madison Avenue, New York, NY 10010-3690

94061QD(0695)MLIC-LD

INVESTMENT SELECTION

Since its passage in 1993, Section 404(c) has spurred many plan sponsors to consider carefully the number and types of investment options they offer their participants: voluntary compliance with 404(c) regulations gives plan sponsors of individually directed 401(k) accounts limited liability protection against losses resulting from participants' investment decisions. One of its key requirements is that plan sponsors offer a minimum of three investment options, each of which has distinctly different risk/reward characteristics.

Some plan sponsors who comply with 404(c) overestimate its protection. None can afford to become complacent simply because it complies. Under most circumstances, *plan sponsors still bear primary responsibility for*:

➤ determining what investment alternatives to offer,

➤ selecting the investment managers or funds,

➤ monitoring performance,

➤ distributing timely information about investment options, and

➤ processing participant investment changes promptly and accurately.

Many experts believe that *how* sponsors fulfill these responsibilities has more serious legal implications for liability exposure than the *number and types* of funds they offer.

ERISA "BEST INTEREST" REQUIREMENTS

In selecting funds and investment managers, 401(k) plan administrators must comply with ERISA's basic fiduciary requirements for all qualified retirement plans: these decisions must be made *solely in the best interest* of the participants.

ERISA's "best interest" requirement relates chiefly to investment-related decisions. With participant-directed retirement plans such as 401(k)s, potential conflicts of interest have diminished greatly. However, non-investment "best interest" decisions made by the plan sponsor could conceivably be challenged. For example, couldn't providing for timely, accurate account statements—a consideration in the sponsor's choice of service provider—be interpreted as a decision involving participants' best interests? If ERISA were drafted today, how would it address such non-investment, but nonetheless consequential, issues?

Investment managers are often selected for the wrong reasons—those not necessarily in the best financial interests of 401(k) plan participants. Factors such as fees, convenience, and the quality of non-investment services such as recordkeeping, often dominate the decision-making process. In many cases, personal or existing business relationships can influence the selection of investment managers and plan sponsors often make decisions in the justifiable interest of saving money.

Those who deal with complaints from plan participants about untimely, inaccurate statements are right to be concerned about the quality of recordkeeping services. But how many points will you win if your participants receive statements that are distributed on time—but investment performance is below par? If your participants file lawsuits because they incur investment losses, how will a court view your apparent interest in non-investment related issues? The attorney representing your participants will likely prove that you could have structured your plan to give participants *both* timely, accurate statements *and* satisfactory investment results.

Investment performance should be the most important factor in your investment manager selection. Higher fees can be acceptable if the manager's performance is consistently good.

An Alternative to Off-the-Shelf Funds

Investment performance and a sharper focus on plan expenses become increasingly important as a plan grows.

For some popular funds, investment fees exceed 100 basis points (1%). Why should a large 401(k) plan generating substantial investment volume pay the same fee as small individual investors? Some astute plan sponsors have cut investment expenses by having their fund manager run an individual portfolio that mirrors its registered fund. As the size of the plan's portfolio increases, the investment management fees decrease, unlike fees for registered funds which usually remain constant regardless of how much a 401(k) invests in them. *Reducing the investment management fee by only 25 basis points will boost participant accumulations by approximately 5% over a 20-year period.*

Establish Written Investment Policies

Defined benefit plan administrators would never dream of beginning a manager search without a written investment policy. Yet many 401(k) plans operate without one. You can reduce your liability exposure significantly by establishing a written investment policy for each type of investment fund your plan offers. This policy statement can guide manager searches and quarterly performance analysis, as well as help you determine when it's time to change managers.

Internal Teamwork Helps Find the Best Service Provider

At many companies the selection of service providers, including the investment manager, is chiefly the responsibility of the human resources staff. The quality of services like recordkeeping and employee communication has long driven their decision-making process because selling the plan to employees is a major concern. Investment performance may be less of a consideration because the company's financial results are not affected by the investment returns of the 401(k) plan and, in light of their own limited investment expertise, it seems a lower priority to many human resources professionals.

Many companies recognize the wisdom of pooling the expertise of a financial officer or defined benefit plan administrator with their 401(k) plan administrator for important plan decision-making such as the selection of a service provider.

At R.R. Donnelley & Sons,[18] Jack Moore, Assistant Treasurer, and Dewey Ingham, Vice President of Compensation and Benefits, worked as a team to increase the fund options for their 401(k) plan.

Together they identified potential investment managers through their own research, and with help from their pension consultant who distributed a questionnaire to the prospective managers and suggested finalists who met the standards Moore and Ingham established. The two then made on-site visits to every finalist. Moore handled the investment due diligence and Ingham evaluated the candidates' recordkeeping and participant-support capabilities.

After helping to expand the 401(k) plan options from one to eight funds, Moore continues to contribute his investment expertise by monitoring performance. What makes this teamwork so successful, Moore contends, is that he and Ingham began and continue to work together with a high level of trust and respect for one another's capabilities.

If you do not have asset management expertise in-house, it's a good idea to retain the services of an independent, fee-based consultant. This will not only reduce your liability exposure, but help to improve your participants' investment performance. The cost of this service can be borne by the plan.

If your participants ever sue your company as a result of unfavorable investment performance, your manager search, selection and firing process will be carefully scrutinized. You must be able to demonstrate that your company conducted all selection processes through thorough, professional due diligence: *keep a good paper trail.*

SELECTING INVESTMENT OPTIONS

Typically, 401(k) plans now offer between four and twelve funds, more than the three stipulated as a minimum for 404(c) regulatory compliance. All plan sponsors should consider offering a range of funds that will help participants diversify their portfolios.

In 1994 AT&T[19] doubled investment options for its $10 billion 401(k) plan, one of the largest in the country, which covers 91,000 non-union administrative and management employees. Now participants can choose from three AT&T custom funds, three investment strategy funds, three registered mutual funds and a company stock fund. Each of the investment strategy funds has pre-defined allocation ranges and includes both U.S. and non-U.S. securities.

---

[18] Chicago-based R.R. Donnelley & Sons Company, Inc. is the largest printer in North America with total 401(k) plan assets of $300 million and 15,000 participants.

[19] AT&T has total plan assets of $10 billion and 91,000 participants representing 89% of eligible employees.

AT&T 401(k) PLAN INVESTMENT OPTIONS			
INVESTMENT STRATEGY	ASSET ALLOCATION	NORMAL MIX	ALLOCATION RANGE
Conservative	Equity	20%	0% - 40%
	Fixed-income	80%	60% - 80%
Moderate	Equity	50%	30% - 70%
	Fixed-income	50%	30% - 70%
Aggressive	Equity	80%	60% - 100%
	Fixed-income	20%	0% - 40%

AT&T's range of investment options is based on both participant input and sound investment principles, according to James Heller, Vice President of savings plans and other post-employment benefits. Heller explains: "With a plan the size of AT&T's, participants have a wide range of investment experience and skill. Some prefer to customize their own asset mix, which the combination of custom funds and mutual funds allows them to do. Many others are less comfortable making their own investment allocation decisions. The investment strategy fund options enable them to put this responsibility in the hands of a professional, if they so choose."

 S M A R T   P I L L S

> Remember: it's your fiduciary responsibility under ERISA to select investment options that are in the best financial interest of your plan participants.

> Beware of potential conflicts that could arise from existing business or personal relationships between your company and service providers.

> To minimize liability, establish a written investment policy for each type of investment fund you offer and use it to select funds and monitor performance.

> Capitalize on in-house investment expertise and collaborations for plan conversions, manager searches and monitoring of investment performance.

> If your company has no internal investment expertise, consider hiring a professional consultant as a plan expense.

> Consider having your fund manager mirror an off-the-shelf fund at a reduced management fee.

401(K) **C** OMPLETE

It's about people

401(K) COMPLETE℠ SERVICES
Investment Options from MainStay and other Fund Families*
Employee Communications and Education
Participant Service Center
Recordkeeping and Administration
Plan Design and Consulting
Trustee Services

Younger people. Older people. People with diverse retirement needs. Your 401(k) plan has to work for all employees by providing an easy way for them to understand what your plan is all about. And how to get the most from it.

After all, a 401(k) plan isn't about numbers.

It's about people.

NYL Benefit Services Company
A New York Life Company

Call 1-800-586-1413

CHAPTER FOUR

SERVICE PROVIDER SELECTION

According to Bob Wuelfing, President of Access Research, Inc.,[20] internal expenses within the 401(k) service provider market now exceed billed service fees by $75 million annually. He estimates services for an additional four million participants are necessary to erase these losses. Despite the fact that the 401(k) market continues to expand, there simply is not enough market share for the survival of all of today's largest service providers. Wuelfing predicts that in the not-too-distant future, a major industry consolidation will result in the control of 80% of total market revenues by the 15 largest service providers, with hundreds of niche players competing for the remaining 20% of market share.

The current abundance of service providers has both a positive and negative impact on plan sponsors. Competitive pressures force providers to offer more services at lower prices in order to get and retain clients. Poor financial results, however, have caused some service providers to leave the business and others—often unexpectedly—to terminate unprofitable client relationships.

Service provider instability is a much more serious problem for a 401(k) plan than it is for other types of qualified retirement plans. If the organization performing the actuarial valuation for your defined benefit pension plan exits this business, finding a new provider for your next actuarial valuation is merely an inconvenience. Plan operations, such as the issuance of checks to pensioners, will continue uninterrupted. In contrast, if your 401(k) service provider goes out of the business, your entire plan operations could come to a screeching halt and cause an irreparable loss of confidence among your participants.

Each plan sponsor must consider how the likely shakeout of service providers will affect its own 401(k) plan: you don't want to be caught by surprise if your provider suddenly abandons the business or drops you as a client. During a meeting

---

[20] Access Research, Inc., headquartered in Windsor, CT, is a leading source of information on service provider trends, and has conducted extensive studies for members of The Society of Professional Administrators and Recordkeepers (SPARK) who handle the recordkeeping for virtually the entire 401(k) market.

with the service provider for one of his company's plans in August 1993, Al Malagiere, Manager of Qualified Retirement Plans at CDI[21] was informed that the last valuation the company would perform would be in September. At the time, the plan covered about 2200 participants and had assets of more than $20 million. Fortunately, CDI had recently conducted a search to find one service provider who could manage all of their 401(k) plans, so they were able to move to a new provider without serious problems. Other plan sponsors who find themselves in the same situation may not be as lucky.

How can you minimize the risk of selecting or retaining a service provider who may abandon you? As you review service providers, make sure you have satisfactory answers to the following critical questions:

☑ 1. How long has the service provider been in the 401(k) business? Avoid a new entrant whose management team lacks experience unless you want to be the guinea pig.

☑ 2. Why is the service provider in the 401(k) business? Is this its primary business or is it a spin-off? If 401(k) management is not its primary business, how does it fit in with its strategic plan? What percentage of its total business comes from 401(k) services?

☑ 3. Who are the owners of the business? If it is privately owned, are the principal shareholders nearing retirement age? If it is a publicly owned company, is it a candidate for a takeover?

☑ 4. How many staff members are dedicated to the 401(k) business? How many did the service provider have at the end of each of the last three years? Has it recently reduced its staff through layoffs—or does it plan to do so?

☑ 5. Does the service provider have an impressive client list? What are the sizes of the companies it services? What is the total number of plan participants and assets? How many clients did it gain and lose during each of the last three years? And why?

☑ 6. What are the service provider's marketing strategies and philosophies? Does it have a dedicated client services group to support your 401(k) business properly? How does it plan to help you increase enrollment?

☑ 7. Does the service provider have the resources to sustain the necessary investments in new technology?

☑ 8. What product enhancements has it made during the last three years, and how much capital does it plan to commit for future enhancements? How much does it invest in new technology?

☑ 9. Does the service provider have a promising market niche? What is its long-term strategy for survival and growth in the face of a service provider shakeout?

It could be difficult to get satisfactory answers to all of these questions, especially

---

[21] Based in Philadelphia, CDI is the largest U.S. provider of temporary technical personnel with total 401(k) plan assets of $64 million and 10,000 participants.

from a privately owned company. The fact that a service provider is not publicly owned, however, does not mean it cannot provide information about its operating results. If a service provider claims this information is unavailable, you should be concerned about its financial management.

An on-site visit with the people who will service your plan and a tour of their processing center are good ideas. Is the staff well-trained, committed, motivated?

Once you are satisfied that you have found a financially stable service provider who is committed to the business, the next step is to determine if it is a good match for your plan.

THE 401(k) SERVICE PROVIDER ALLIANCE

There has been an increased demand among 401(k) plan sponsors for bundled provider services so that investment management, recordkeeping and plan consulting are available from one source. Service providers who do not manage funds, for example, have been forced to form alliances with investment managers in order to compete with major mutual fund companies.

The potential loss of independence and objectivity in an alliance has been a source of much controversy. How can consultants, for example, serve as independent advisors and help plan sponsors select the best providers if the same consultants are expected to sell their own firms' products and services?

If you plan to use an alliance for your 401(k) plan management, you ought to find out how much business the alliance has generated in total, and for each of the providers involved. Any business alliance must be profitable for *all of the providers* in order to survive over the long-term.

Another issue to consider is that alliances are often formed through personal relationships, and in many cases several individuals invest a significant amount of personal capital to create the alliance. If one or more individuals leave the alliance, will others commit the same resources? Because alliances are relatively new to the 401(k) business, it is difficult to predict what will happen if and when an alliance folds. You need to feel comfortable that your alliance has the financial, personal—and group—commitment to stay together over the long-term.

LOOK FOR SIGNS OF TROUBLE

Because the future of the 401(k) service provider market is, at best, uncertain, you should meet with your service provider at least once a year. Do not assume everything is fine just because your plan appears to be running smoothly. Look for early warning signs that your current provider may be heading for trouble.

Ed Fenton, Retirement Plan Administrator of New Jersey Transit[22] said his plan acted before they were acted on: "We knew our provider was going through a turbulent period when the people assigned to our plan and the computer reports kept changing and we had no face-to-face contact. Their competitors confirmed that they were having problems and we prepared early for a change."

Perhaps the single most important question you can ask your service provider is

---

[22] New Jersey Transit, based in Newark, has total 401(k) plan assets of $57 million and 1,600 participants representing 89% of eligible employees.

whether your company is viewed as a profitable client. If it isn't, will you be dropped when there is pressure to improve financial results? Can the service provider handle your plan comfortably? Have they promised more than they can deliver? The better you understand your service provider's present and future goals and capabilities, the greater the likelihood that your plan will actually benefit from long-term, top-quality service.

 S M A R T   P I L L S

> Watch for signs—such as staff turnover—that your service provider may be financially unstable.

> Make sure your service provider is committed to 401(k) plan management as an integral part of its business.

> Meet with your service provider at least once a year to determine whether it is taking the necessary steps to keep pace with new technology.

> Speak to a variety of service providers to get an insider's perspective on the strength and viability of your own record-keeper—and others you may be considering.

LOANS

The 401(k) plan loan provision continues to be a hotly debated issue. Equal numbers of plans do and do not allow loans. Supporters of loan provisions believe loans are necessary in order to obtain and sustain adequate plan participation but there is little, if any, data to support that conclusion. Most 401(k) plans have so many other features that loan provisions may not be necessary in order to obtain high participant levels. Very few employees will forego participation in a plan that has a 25% to 50% matching employer contribution simply because the plan does not permit loans.

The real issue is whether a loan provision is right for your plan. For businesses that have high turnover and short-term breaks in service, loan administration is particularly troublesome because continuous loan payments are required to avoid a taxable default. Since it is difficult to withdraw a loan benefit once it is in place, be sure to address each of these issues as you develop a loan provision:

A LOAN PROVISION CHECKLIST

✓ 1. How will the loan provision be communicated to plan participants?

✓ 2. How will your plan handle the Department of Treasury requirement that participants must borrow the maximum amount from their 401(k) plans before hardship withdrawals are permitted?

✓ 3. Will loans be permitted for any reason, or for only specific purposes such as buying a home? Who will decide whether the loan has been requested for a valid purpose?

✓ 4. For loans that are used to purchase a home, will the maximum loan term be limited to five years?

✓ 5. Will more than one loan be permitted per participant? If so, how many?

✓ 6. What participant collateral will secure loans?

✓ 7. Who will be responsible for the loan modeling? Who will prepare the amortization schedule?

✓ 8. Who will prepare the promissory note and other loan documents?

✓ 9. Will loans be repaid only through payroll deductions?

✓ 10. How is the loan payment schedule affected if the participant is temporarily laid-off or on an unpaid leave of absence?

✓ 11. What happens when participants who have outstanding loan balances leave the company? If these participants leave their 401(k) account balances in your plan, will they be kept on a monthly loan payment schedule or will there be automatic acceleration? Will these participants be permitted to take out new loans?

✓ 12. How will the interest rate be established and will it be fixed or variable?

✓ 13. How often will the interest rate for new loans be adjusted?

✓ 14. Will each loan be considered an asset assigned to the participant's account, or will loans be combined into a general loan fund?

✓ 15. Will loans be initiated through manual paperwork, or after participants call a voice response unit?

✓ 16. How will loan payments be invested in the plan?

✓ 17. Will participants be able to select the investment fund(s) from which the loan withdrawal will be made, or will plan provisions dictate a withdrawal priority order?

✓ 18. From which contribution sources, such as employee pre-tax and employer matching funds, and in what order, will the borrowed money be taken?

✓ 19. Will participants be charged a fee for setting up the loan in addition to an annual administrative fee?

Before you establish a loan provision, make sure your recordkeeper can provide the administrative support you need. The biggest problem Ed Fenton, Retirement Plan Administrator, New Jersey Transit[23] experienced when he was forced to find a new recordkeeper centered on loan record transfers. Initially, NJT's loan administration was handled outside the recordkeeping system; as a result, the participant records transfer tape that was given to the new recordkeeper did not include the loan information. Considerable time and effort were required to obtain it.

One way to make loan provisions more manageable is to limit participants to one loan at a time. If a participant with an outstanding loan wants to borrow more, the outstanding balance and the new amount borrowed could be combined into one new loan. The new loan payments must be structured so that the original loan will be paid off within the original loan term to avoid negative tax consequences.

If your current loan provision has serious administrative problems, you may want to consider tightening up your procedures for all or only new plan participants. It

---

[23] New Jersey Transit, based in Newark, has total 401(k) plan assets of $57 million and 1,600 participants representing 89% of eligible employees.

may be wise to avoid the problems that may be created by introducing a more restrictive loan policy to only new participants. Check with your professional advisors, however, to see if different loan provisions for old and new participants are likely to raise compliance issues.

SMART PILLS

➤ To avoid administrative headaches, carefully plan a new loan provision.

➤ Before you add a loan provision to your plan, talk to other plan sponsors to learn from their good and bad experiences.

➤ Make sure your recordkeeper can provide proper administrative support for a loan provision.

➤ If you have administrative problems with your current loan provision, consider tightening up the procedures for new participants.

'We can't imagine Fidelity providing better 401(k) service to a big corporation. But the way we're growing, we'll eventually find out."

Birgitt Wirth, Benefits Manager, IKEA

◆ ◆ ◆ ◆ ◆

When IKEA went hunting for a better 401(k), they wanted to be sure that they, and their employees, would be important to their new provider. "When Fidelity said they had a division dedicated to small and mid-sized companies, and that we'd be one of their largest clients, their size was no longer an issue," said Birgitt Wirth, Benefits Manager.

This made IKEA's switch to The CORPORATEplan *for Retirement* – an integrated and coordinated service, all under one roof and only available directly from Fidelity – comfortable right from the start. "Fidelity is very customer service oriented. In fact, it's the best customer service I've ever had," Wirth said.

"Fidelity's enrollment and implementation programs were terrific. But their ongoing support and education has been, too. The STAGES® communications program, the Strategy Selector™ Software, the 800 number support staff – all first class."

And you think, Ms. Wirth, even a big corporation wouldn't get better service? "No, I don't. But ask me again in a few years."

Your retirement plan. Our full time job.

The CORPORATEplan *for Retirement* is designed for small to mid-sized companies. It is backed by a business unit within Fidelity whose every activity is guided by a single purpose: to help all of our customers – from the benefits manager to the most recent plan participant – reach their retirement goals. If you want this level of commitment behind your plan, call Fidelity for a free brochure at 1-800-343-9184. Your retirement plan is our full time job.

1-800-343-9184 Ext. 8423

CHAPTER SIX

SPOUSAL WAIVERS

The Retirement Equity Act of 1984 (REA) requires the participant's spouse to consent to the naming of another person as the beneficiary of the participant's 401(k) account, by signing a spousal waiver. In an age of multiple marriages and complex family relationships, several aspects of this law can create significant liability exposure for corporate plan sponsors.

The first liability risk involves the signatures that appear on the spousal waiver. REA requires that the signing of the waiver be witnessed either by a plan representative or a notary. It is legal, and usually most convenient, for a plan representative to sign as the witness. But an employee who wants to name a non-spouse as the beneficiary might not resist the temptation to have an imposter sign for the spouse. Avoid this potentially dangerous situation by requiring the waiver signing to be witnessed by a notary whose job it is to verify that the person signing has been properly identified.

PHONY SPOUSAL WAIVERS

If a participant submits a phony spousal waiver, the plan sponsor may become entangled in a legal embroglio between the named beneficiary and the spouse. In the worst case, the spouse's claim will be filed after the account balance has already been paid to the beneficiary. You may be forced to pay the spouse and recover the amount you paid to the named beneficiary.

Changes in the marital status of participants can create a potential conflict, as well. For example: assume an employee is a single parent when he or she joins the plan and the children are named as beneficiaries. When the participant remarries, a new beneficiary designation is not submitted. The participant dies and the children expect to receive the 401(k) account balance. Legally, the new spouse became the beneficiary at the moment vows were exchanged regardless of what is on file in your records. Several problems could arise: you might pay the children inadvertently; the spouse could submit a claim after you have paid the children; or, you may become involved in a legal battle between the spouse and the children before the benefit is paid. It is likely that you will be forced to pay the spouse. But the children can sue you for failing to notify the participant of the need to file a new beneficiary form.

Some participants attempt to avoid these problems with a prenuptial agreement that includes a waiver of 401(k) benefits. To date, most courts have considered this waiver ineffective, however, because the person signing a spousal waiver in a prenuptial agreement is not yet an actual spouse. REA specifically requires the waiver of the spouse.

Representative Nancy Johnson (R-CT) has introduced new legislation at the suggestion of The 401(k) Association that permits prenuptial agreements in beneficiary disputes. In the meantime, it is a good idea to discuss spousal waivers in your summary plan description and send reminders to participants at least once a year.

To reduce your liability exposure with regard to spousal waivers:

➤ Ask participants to submit a new beneficiary form if their marital status has changed.

➤ Advise participants who have entered into prenuptial agreements to submit a new beneficiary form with a proper spousal waiver once they are married.

➤ Remind participants to change their 401(k) plan beneficiaries when they request a change of beneficiary form for group life insurance, or when they change from single to family medical coverage.

Even if you have a spousal waiver on file, consider requiring the spouse's signature again before distributing money from the participant's account to a non-spouse. If the participant has died, check to make sure the actual spouse has signed the waiver.

 NOTE: *REA rules regarding spouses apply to any distribution (except a joint-and-survivor annuity that has the current spouse as the beneficiary), even "direct rollover" distributions to an IRA or another employer-sponsored qualified retirement plan.*

Problems related to REA will increase as plans mature and account balances rise. Make sure you understand all the issues surrounding spousal waivers—and communicate them clearly to your participants.

S M A R T   P I L L S

➤ To reduce your company's liability exposure, require participants to have a notary, rather than a plan representative, witness the spousal waiver signing.

➤ Inform all participants of REA spousal waiver requirements at least once a year.

➤ Watch for changes in marital status that affect spousal waivers on forms for group life insurance beneficiaries and medical coverage.

➤ Even if you have a spousal waiver on file, consider requiring the spouse's signature again before money is distributed from a participant's account.

C H A P T E R
SEVEN

Qualified Domestic Relations Orders
(QDROs)

The Retirement Equity Act of 1984 permits the ex-spouse of a participant to file a Qualified Domestic Relations Order (QDRO) in order to claim all or part of his or her 401(k) account balance after a divorce is final. The ex-spouse has the same rights to his or her portion of the account as any other participant. Extreme caution must be exercised when dealing with the sticky issue of QDROs.

One of the biggest problems for plan sponsors is that most divorce attorneys know little or nothing about qualified retirement plans. As a result, many of the QDROs filed on behalf of an ex-spouse continue to include impermissible or administratively impossible provisions. Granting a benefit to an ex-spouse based on a defective QDRO could create a liability problem for your company because the participant could claim that the payment should never have been made. Make certain the QDRO is correct before you accept it. If no one within your organization is familiar with QDRO requirements, get outside professional help.

Sally Gottlieb, Benefits Manager of Apple Computer[24], retained the services of a divorce attorney to draft a procedural checklist for QDROs. This checklist is given to the employee and the ex-spouse, along with a sample order that explains the allocation of investment gains and losses and the tax penalties related to distributions to the ex-spouse. Even so, Apple's legal department still spends a lot of time discussing QDROs with employees and outside attorneys. Gottlieb notes that it is difficult for their legal department to serve two clients: the company and the employee. This new procedure has made it easier for employees and their legal counsel to develop an accurate QDRO and expedite its settlement.

Gottlieb has seen defective QDROs that do not mention the plan by name, or that request a monthly annuity when the plan isn't set up to provide annuities. Another common defect is a request from the ex-spouse's attorney to split the

---

[24] Apple Computer, based in Cupertino, CA, has total 401(k) plan assets of $160 million and 8,000 participants representing 87% of eligible employees.

account as of a certain date—an impossibility if the account is not valued daily and the date specified is not a valuation date.

You must decide if a participant's account should be frozen when a defective QDRO has been filed (or in some cases, when the divorce proceedings begin, if the plan receives a "notice of joinder" or similar domestic relations court filing) so that its money cannot be withdrawn until the matter is resolved. If, for example, you allow the participant to withdraw any amount from the account, the ex-spouse may file suit claiming the withdrawal should not have been permitted when there was a pending divorce settlement. Refusing to make the distribution will infuriate the employee and may be difficult legally if there is no established policy. This illustrates the conflict Gottlieb pointed out when plan administrators are forced to choose between protecting the company's and the participant's interests.

While the topic of 401(k) participant divorces may seem more family than company-related, QDROs are a major issue facing today's plan sponsors; Pacific Gas & Electric, for example, has prepared a booklet on the subject. All plan sponsors should consider some form of communication on this important matter.

☞ **NOTE:** *Under a 1994 Department of Labor ruling, a plan's legal costs in connection with a QDRO cannot be charged to a participant's account, although in most cases they can be charged to the plan as a whole.*

S M A R T   P I L L S

➤ Learn about QDROs before you have to deal with one.

➤ Establish policies and procedures in advance so you don't struggle when you get your first QDRO.

➤ Make sure the QDRO is accurate and complete before you accept it.

➤ Retain outside professional help if your staff is unfamiliar with QDROs.

RETIREMENT

SHOULD BE

CAREFREE.

SO SHOULD

MANAGING

A COMPANY

401(k) PLAN.

Giving your participants the resources to retire well. That's the goal of every plan manager. But who can make the management process easy for you?

LaSalle National Trust can. When you work with LaSalle, you have the advantage of your own LaSalle Manager who will give you the flexible strategies and the timely information you and your participants need to make sound decisions.

But our service doesn't stop there. We also design personalized communications for your company, train your employees, even provide you with our financial planning interactive computer disc.

In short, you get the same sophisticated support that the largest providers of 401(k) services offer to the largest corporations. To put us to work for you, call Bob Hudon, Senior Vice President, at (312) 904-2495 or 2413. And let go of a few more of your cares.

LaSalle National Trust, N.A.

WHAT PLAN PARTICIPANTS
WANT TO KNOW ABOUT 401(k) PLANS

How many times are you asked the same question about your company's 401(k) plan? Despite your knowledge and expertise, don't you often search for simple ways to explain the complex details embedded in your plan? No matter how many times you field even the most basic question, you know you can't give any inquiry short shrift; a clear, accurate and comprehensive answer is vital to each of your participants and eligible enrollees.

This Q&A Section has been thoroughly researched and written to provide practical answers to those questions most commonly asked about 401(k) plans. We hope it will become a dog-eared bible for newer staff members with little or no 401(k) experience, and a trusted guide for seasoned plan administrators who often need a single, convenient source of comprehensive information. It gives you in-depth, hard-to-find explanations in understandable, layman's language, and clarifies issues that are important—but often overlooked—by participants and plan administrators alike.

Many of the charts, illustrations and explanations appear in the Investors Press sister publication **Building Your Nest Egg With Your 401(k)**, written by Lynn Brenner *specifically for plan participants and eligible enrollees*. **Nest Egg** emphasizes the importance of saving—early and to the maximum extent possible. Many key concepts, like the magic of compounding and the relentless impact of inflation, are explained and more than one hundred questions are answered in language that is easy for a typical plan participant to understand.

The questions and answers included in this 401(k) Administrator's Guide identify critical issues that you and your staff members must address to meet regulatory requirements and help your employees achieve retirement security. Since the questions reflect a wide range of participant concerns, *you may need to tailor your answers to the specific provisions of your plan.*

Because our goal is to balance the technical with the practical, there are three important things to keep in mind as you read these questions and answers:

➤ The questions are asked *as if the participant were speaking to you.* The answers *are given to you* to help frame your response to the participant.

➤ The *responses do not cover* all applicable laws and regulations. Federal laws and regulations change frequently; you need to check current statutes as they apply to your plan provisions.

➤ Because of these frequent changes, figures listed may need updating in successive years.

THE FOLLOWING TEN CHAPTERS WILL COVER THESE KEY AREAS:

CHAPTER ONE

CONTRIBUTIONS

 How much of my pay can I contribute to my 401(k) plan?
In 1995, *the maximum pre-tax dollar amount* a participant can make
is $9,240—subject to the 25% of pay limitation and the special non-
discrimination test described below.

This government-imposed dollar ceiling is determined by laws and regulations
issued by the Treasury Department and administered through the Internal
Revenue Service. Your plan has probably established specific contribution limits
which may be lower, designed to meet compliance as easily as possible.

The Tax Reform Act of 1986 established a $7,000 maximum limit to reduce
the loss of annual tax revenue to Uncle Sam. The legal limit for contributions has
risen annually to reflect cost of living increases. The 1994 GATT trade law
changed the way this limit is determined: starting in 1995, increases will be made
in increments of only $500. At the current inflation rate, that means an increase
every two years rather than every year. This change will effectively slow the
growth of the maximum contribution amount.

The percentage of pay limit for contributions is more complex. The amount that
can be accumulated in all of an employee's tax-qualified defined contribution
plans—not just in the 401(k)—is limited to a total of 25% of pay or $30,000,
whichever is less. This limit applies to all employees, regardless of income level.
Every contribution dollar counts, employer's and employee's alike.

To make matters more complicated, the 25% limit includes contributions
forfeited by employees who have left the company prior to full vesting if those
contributions are re-allocated among the remaining employee accounts and if, in
calculating the percentage, "pay" (the denominator of the percentage fraction) is
reduced by salary deferrals and pre-tax contributions to a Section 125 plan.

To fall safely within regulatory compliance, most plans stipulate a specific
percentage of pay their participants can contribute, ranging from 1% to 15%.
Where plans set the limit depends on the number and type of benefits they offer
that feature pre-tax contributions. Participants can choose their contribution
percentage within the total percentage allowed by their plan.

EXAMPLE

Employee Sally Stock earns $30,000; she contributes 15% of her gross pay to her company 401(k), and $100 pre-tax per month toward her medical coverage:

Gross income:	$30,000
Pre-tax medical contribution:	$ 1,200
Employee 401(k) contribution:	$ 4,500
Compensation after pre-tax contribution:	$24,300

25% percent of Sally's $24,300 compensation after pre-tax contributions comes to a maximum allowable contribution limit of $6,075. In this example, the company could contribute up to an additional $1,575 ($6,075 - $4,500) to Sally's account.

EXAMPLE

A company with no employee pre-tax contribution arrangement for medical benefits, no employer 401(k) match, or no other tax-qualified retirement plan may allow its employees to contribute as much as 20% of their compensation to their 401(k) account. (20% of gross pay will equal 25% of after-tax pay.)

Gross income	$30,000
Less employee 401(k) contribution (20% of gross income)	$ 6,000
Compensation after 401(k) contributions	$24,000

25% of the remaining $24,000 of compensation is equal to the 20% employee contribution.

Conversely, a company with pre-tax employee contributions for medical coverage, employee-funded dependent care accounts, employer contributions to the 401(k) plan or a defined benefit pension plan might limit its employee 401(k) contributions to only 10% of compensation to guarantee that no employee exceeds the 25% maximum contribution limit.

How Do Companies Set Contribution Limits?

Setting contribution limits is much like balancing on a high-wire buffeted by gale-storm winds. You might set your company limit at what seems a "safe" level, but if *even one* employee exceeds the Federal limits test, your company might jeopardize its tax-qualified status. This risk must be weighed against your overall goals of helping participants reach adequate retirement savings and achieving the highest possible participation levels.

The tricky part in determining the company limit is deriving an unknown variable from an unknown; it's difficult to know whether your limit is too high until you know the consequences. The Federal 25% limit is calculated against an employee's earnings after the employee's pre-tax contributions are made to any applicable plans—401(k), medical, and so forth. You must deduct the employee's pre-tax contribution from the gross earnings to arrive at the amount subject to the 25% limit, but to do that you need to have a percentage limit on which to base the employee's pre-tax contribution.

As a result, limiting employee pre-tax contributions to only 10% or less of compensation may reduce needlessly the amount most employees would be permitted to contribute. It also may make it more difficult to pass the 401(k) non-discrimination test because many non-highly compensated employees (non-HCEs) are restricted to a lower contribution percentage. Therefore, most plan sponsors will establish a higher contribution percentage and then closely monitor contributions to make sure this limit is not exceeded.

Remember the penalty if even one employee exceeds this limit: *potential disqualification of your plan.*[1] Many service providers do not conduct proper Section 415 limitation tests; make sure your provider, consultant or plan administrator is using compensation after all pre-tax contributions. And remember: additional Section 415(e) limitation testing is necessary for employers who offer a defined benefit plan and a defined contribution plan.

 Consider the dependent care account. Generally, few employees take advantage of this benefit; many prefer to take the Federal tax credit when they file their income taxes. But for those who use the benefit, it often represents a considerable chunk of their pre-tax pay. If a company structures its contribution percentage limit around this benefit, it has to limit the 401(k) contribution amount substantially, possibly driving everyone's limit below the level necessary for adequate retirement savings.

How little of my pay can I contribute?

There's *no legal minimum* contribution, but most plans establish a minimum equal to 1% or 2% of the participant's pay. A percentage of pay is an easier deduction at each pay period than specific dollar amounts.

Are 401(k) contributions deducted from all of my compensation?

It depends on your plan's rules and on how much the participant earns. When a plan is established, the employer can include all compensation—overtime, bonuses, commissions and shift differentials—or only a portion, such as base pay, when determining total compensation.

 NOTE: *If your plan does not include total compensation, it will be required to pass an additional non-discrimination test each year to qualify for tax-deferred status.*

Is it true that if I earn over a certain amount, my contributions are capped?

Yes. In addition to the 25% limit, the Federal government has set special contribution limits for highly compensated employees (HCEs). What is Uncle Sam's definition of highly paid? Complicated regulations determine this. In 1995, it is generally anyone earning more than $66,000 per year, or whose total compensation puts them in the top-paid 20% of the company's employees. Federal non-discrimination rules prevent HCEs from saving a substantially greater percentage of their pay in the 401(k) than non-HCEs can.

Federal non-discrimination rules are monstrously complex, but they allow plan administrators some latitude in how they test.

---

[1] Section 415 was added to the Internal Revenue Code when ERISA was passed. Among other things, it established maximum annual combined employer/employee 401(k) contributions. Recently, the potential for disqualification for minor infractions of Section 415(e) rules has been mitigated by new IRS compliance programs.

Pre-tax contributions must meet one of the following tests:

1. The average contribution percentage for HCEs must not exceed 1.25 times the average percentage for the non-HCEs.

2. The average contribution percentage for HCEs must not exceed two percentage points above the average compensation percentage for non-HCEs, and the average contribution percentage for HCEs must not be more than two times the average contribution percentage for non-HCEs.

The average percentage HCEs will be permitted to contribute will always be controlled by the average percentage the non-HCEs contribute. The following table shows how these tests work for various average contribution percentages:

AVERAGE CONTRIBUTION %	
NON-HCEs	HCEs
1%	2.00%
2	4.00
3	5.00
4	6.00
5	7.00
6	8.00
7	9.00
8	10.00
9	11.25
10	12.50
11	13.75
12	15.00

As a result of this test, most plans typically allow HCEs to contribute only 5% or 6% of pay; for an employee earning $70,000 that amounts to about $3,500. This limitation can be frustrating to borderline HCEs who object that employees earning just a few dollars less than they earn can contribute almost three times as much. At some companies, non-HCE participation levels are high enough to preclude restrictions, but generally, HCEs are affected adversely.

Your plan must pass annual non-discrimination tests after the plan year ends. If there's too big a gap between HCE and non-HCE contributions, the plan has to make an adjustment either by refunding part of the contribution made by the HCEs or by making additional employer contributions for all or some of the non-HCEs. Refunds are added back into the HCEs' taxable income.

5 **Are family members who work for the same employer affected by special non-discrimination tests?**

The contributions of a spouse, lineal ascendants and descendants of a highly compensated employee (HCE) may also be limited if they work for the same employer. Do any family members of your HCEs work for your company?

What is the $150,000 compensation limit?

Current law forbids employees from making 401(k) contributions for any compensation over $150,000; they cannot receive matching or other employer contributions for any compensation over this limit. The dollar limit must also be used to determine the employee's contribution percentage for non-discrimination testing purposes. It is adjusted periodically: in 1993 it was lowered from $235,840 to the current limit.

Satisfying the discrimination test is a major reason why plan sponsors attempt to achieve the highest possible participation levels. To compensate for the restrictions of the non-discrimination rules and the $150,000 compensation cap, many plan sponsors offer non-qualified plans to allow highly compensated employees (HCEs) to set aside larger amounts on a tax-favored basis.

NOTE: *Employer matching contributions and employee after-tax contributions are also subject to discrimination testing. In some cases, employers can use fully vested employer contributions to help satisfy the test.*

 When can I change my contribution percentage?

Most 401(k) plans permit contribution changes on specific dates, usually the beginning of each month, or each calendar quarter. Although some plans permit changes at any time, most employers limit the frequency to avoid excessive administrative costs.

What happens if I stop contributing to the plan? If I stop, when can I start contributing again?

Although they have no legal obligation to do so, most plans permit employees to stop contributing at any time. Some plans, however, lock each participant into their specified contribution percentage for a full plan year.

Check your plan's rules.

 Typically, participants who suspend contributions are permitted to begin contributing again on any date new employees can enter the plan. But those who stop making contributions because of a hardship withdrawal may have to stay out for at least one full year, depending on the plan's provisions. (See "Hardship Withdrawals," page 106.)

What is a "matching contribution?"

In a nutshell: it's free money. The employer "matches" the participant's contribution by adding to it. The specific amount of the matching contribution is solely up to the employer. For every $1.00 an employee contributes, the employer might match 25 cents, 50 cents, or more, up to a specified ceiling—usually the first 3% to 6% of pay.

 Assume your plan has a matching rate of 50 cents to the dollar for the first 6% of pay an employee contributes. An employee earning $30,000 would receive $900 in employer matching contributions if he or she contributes $1,800. For any contributions in excess of $1,800 the employee would not receive a company

RISK: YOU CAN'T LIVE WITH IT, YOU CAN'T LIVE WITHOUT IT.

 *It's an inescapable fact of life. But one that is seldom grasped by 401(k) plan participants. They fear risk in part because they understand it only in the narrow context of losing their money.*  *They need to understand that risk can be managed, and that without it, many will have no chance of achieving a financially secure retirement.*  *At T. Rowe Price, we look at investing as a marathon, not a sprint. Our goal is to help employees manage risk by providing them with investment options that can help them achieve long-term financial security. Many of our funds have earned Morningstar's best ratings for risk-adjusted performance. Our asset allocation funds help investors reduce risk while providing the potential to achieve attractive returns.*  *It's only natural to be concerned about risk. But with the right investment firm, maybe your employees will start to think of risk not as a problem, but as an opportunity.*  *If you'd like to learn about how we can help your employees become more confident investors, please call John R. Rockwell at (410) 581-5900.*

Invest With Confidence
T. Rowe Price

match. However, the employee would continue to receive the tax benefits for any contributions in excess of the $1,800.

☞ **NOTE:** *Matching contributions are also subject to special non-discrimination tests. Refer to your tax library for specific guidelines.*

10 **What type of employer contributions are there beside matching cash contributions?**

Some employers offer their match in the form of company stock, which they may add to the company ESOP (Employee Stock Ownership Plan). In this case, the contribution may be called an ESOP contribution rather than a matching contribution. Others provide a profit-sharing or gain-sharing enhancement in their plans through a match based on the company's profit for the year. The matching amount is contributed regularly during the year. The enhancement is contributed in a lump sum after the results for the year have been determined, or it can be used to increase the matching contribution for the following year.

There are other types of employer contributions as well. Most employers who replaced their defined benefit pension plans with 401(k)s offer a contribution ranging between 2% and 5% of pay for all eligible employees, regardless of whether or not they contribute. The amount may vary by age so that older employees receive a larger contribution—a "peace offering," if you will—to help offset any negative feeling they might have about changing to a defined contribution plan.

11 **Is my employer required to contribute to the plan?**

No. There is no legal requirement for companies to contribute to a 401(k) plan. Most do, however, as an added incentive for greater employee participation. Remember, the amount the highly compensated employees (HCEs) may contribute is governed by the average percentage the non-HCEs contribute. An employer matching contribution usually increases the level of participation across the board.

12 **Why does my company contribute to the plan? What's in it for them?**

Even though companies receive tax deductions for their contributions, it still costs money to provide this benefit. So why do employers make them? Most want to provide a competitive retirement plan to help attract and retain valuable employees. Employers also want to help their employees accumulate enough money to maintain a comfortable standard of living in retirement and be less dependent on their company for their retirement security. When a company's retirees live comfortably, its image is enhanced with shareholders and customers—and current and prospective employees.

13 **When must my company invest my contributions?**

Department of Labor regulations require plan sponsors to put employee contributions into the plan in a "timely manner" after they are deducted from the employee's pay. But these regulations do not specify how many days constitute a timely manner, except to say that it must never be more than 90 days. Some employers deposit contributions each payroll period; others make monthly contributions. Deposits made less frequently than monthly are inadequate. If the

Department of Labor ever audits your plan, this is a key area it will examine. Your failure to make timely deposits could result in fines and other penalties.

 14 **Must the company's contributions be deposited in the plan at the same time as my contributions?**

No. Plan sponsors have flexibility regarding their contribution deposits. Companies get a tax deduction for their contributions as long as the funds are deposited by the date the corporate tax return is filed (up to September 15 for a company whose tax year ends on December 31).

Check your plan.

Employer practices vary greatly. Many deposit matching contributions each time employee contributions are put into the plan; others do so monthly, quarterly or annually. Make sure participants understand the timing of contributions so they know what will appear on their statements.

15 **Can I make contributions from my after-tax income?**

Some 401(k) plans permit both pre-tax and after-tax contributions. An after-tax 401(k) contribution doesn't reduce the participant's taxable income, but its earnings remain untaxed until the participant withdraws them. Some employers match after-tax contributions, but in many plans only pre-tax contributions qualify for an employer match.

After-tax contributions occur commonly in plans that began as thrift plans before the advent of the 401(k) in 1978. Saving on a pre-tax basis was added later. After-tax contributions must also satisfy special non-discrimination tests.

16 **If my plan permits both pre-tax and after-tax contributions, which type is best?**

Usually, pre-tax contributions are the most advantageous but the answer depends on the specific needs of the participant and the plan provisions. The primary issue is: immediate tax savings versus easier access to the money.

Participants may withdraw pre-tax contributions before age 59½ only if they experience a qualified financial hardship. The IRS allows a participant to claim financial hardship if money is needed to pay for:

1. college tuition for the participant or a dependent, provided that it's due in the next twelve months;

2. the down payment on a primary residence;

3. unreimbursed medical expenses for the participant or a dependent; or

4. to prevent a foreclosure or eviction from the participant's home.

Other "hardship" definitions, like paying for a funeral, may be plan specific and could invite close scrutiny from the IRS.

Pre-tax withdrawals made before age 59½ incur a 10% penalty tax in addition to income tax on the withdrawn amount. After-tax contributions, however, may be withdrawn from most plans for any reason. Participants won't have to pay any taxes (they already did), except on the investment income. So employees who plan to withdraw money from their 401(k) account for a short-term need—like buying a car—may be better off with after-tax contributions.

TIP: Emphasize to employees that it's not a good long-term strategy to regard their 401(k) accounts as easy-access savings. Even with after-tax contributions, *retirement savings is the ultimate goal of the 401(k)*.

17 Can I contribute to both an IRA and a 401(k)?

Yes. But depending on the size of the participant's salary, IRA contributions may not be tax-deductible.

Under current law, participants in qualified employer-sponsored retirement plans like 401(k)s can only deduct 100% of a $2,000 annual IRA contribution if they are:

a) single and earning less than $25,000, or
b) married filing jointly and together earn less than $40,000.

Participants qualify for a partial deduction on the IRA contribution if they are:

a) single and earn between $25,000 and $35,000, or
b) married filing jointly and together earn between $40,000 and $50,000.

Single employees earning over $35,000 and married employees filing jointly with combined earnings of over $50,000 may contribute $2,000 to an IRA, but it is not tax-deductible.

Of course, even if IRA contributions are non-tax-deductible, their earnings will grow on a tax-deferred basis.

18 If I can't afford to contribute to both my 401(k) and an IRA, which is the better choice?

The 401(k), almost always. The decision is really simple if your plan provides matching contributions and/or if any IRA contributions employees make aren't tax deductible. Before they even think of contributing to an IRA, employees should contribute the maximum amount to their 401(k) that will be matched by the company. The company match is a powerful and unbeatable boost to asset growth that costs the employee absolutely nothing.

Although most 401(k) plans provide access to funds through hardship distributions, the major advantage IRAs have over 401(k)s is immediate, no-questions-asked access to distributions at any age. IRAs cannot compete with the non-taxable loans many 401(k) plans offer, however.

The decision gets tougher when matching contributions are not an issue. But it's easier to save with a 401(k) because contributions are automatically deducted from pay. Saving in an IRA requires an ongoing self-discipline that many people simply don't have.

19 Does participating in the 401(k) plan affect any of my other benefits?

Many benefits—group life insurance, disability, defined benefit pension—are based on the employee's annual pay, so the amount an employee contributes to his or her 401(k) may need to be added back into the participant's salary to be sure it is calculated correctly. The documents for other benefits must also include employee pre-tax contributions as part of the employee's compensation.

Jake Louis earns $50,000 a year and by contributing $2,000 to the 401(k) plan, reduces his taxable income to $48,000. If his group life insurance covers him for twice his salary, he'll have only $96,000 of coverage—unless his 401(k) contribution is included in the calculation and the group life contract defines compensation in this manner.

20 **My spouse and I are both eligible to contribute to 401(k) plans. We can't afford to contribute the maximum amount to both plans. How do we decide how much to contribute to each plan?**

Many different factors need to be considered: the amount of each employer's matching contribution; how soon each spouse will be vested in those matching contributions; how attractive each plan's investment options are; and which plan allows borrowing if the couple is likely to need a loan.

Generally, each spouse should contribute the maximum amount that is matched by their employers. If this is too costly, they should put the maximum amount into the plan that has the higher matching contribution. The more generous match can't be the only consideration, though: if there's a reasonable chance that one spouse may change jobs before being vested, it probably makes more sense to opt for the plan with the lower matching contribution.

Couples should compare the plans carefully. Is there a big difference in the quality or reputation of the fund provider? One plan may feature a greater range of investment choices, or may include investments that have performed better.

NOTE: *Participants need to be very careful when comparing the investment performance of two 401(k) plan accounts to make sure they're looking at truly comparable investments.*

For example, an intermediate-term bond fund and a long-term bond fund are not comparable. Each fund's investment performance should be reviewed for the same time period. Any contributions made during the time period should be subtracted; otherwise, a rising balance in one fund may be attributed to better performance when, in fact, the real reason is simply that more money was contributed to the account.

Finally, if participants anticipate the need to borrow from their 401(k) to cover a major expense such as college tuition or a down payment on a house, a loan feature could be the reason to choose one 401(k) plan over the other.

21 **What does the 401(k) plan cost, and who's paying for it?**

Basically, the plan has two kinds of expenses: *administrative costs* and *investment management fees.*

Administrative costs include fees paid for participant recordkeeping and related services. *Investment management fees* are usually charged as a percentage of the total assets under management. These fees might range from 0.2% to 2% of the assets, depending on the investment manager and the type of investment. (Investment management fees are higher for stock funds than for bond funds, for example.)

Other costs include educational materials that help participants decide how to invest their money. Depending on the plan, these educational expenses may be included among administrative fees.

Who pays? In some plans, the employer pays; in others, costs are shared by the employer and the plan participants; and in others all expenses are paid by plan participants. Each participant's individual share of expenses is automatically subtracted from his or her investment returns. Of course, plan participants may pay less for these services than if they made similar investments outside a 401(k) plan.

TIP: Provide information about plan fees and participants' rights and obligations in your Summary Plan Description.

RIGHT NOW SOMEONE IN YOUR COMPANY WHO DOESN'T KNOW THE DIFFERENCE BETWEEN A STOCK AND A BOND IS DECIDING HOW TO INVEST THEIR 401*K* MONEY.

Perhaps you've seen that blank stare in an employee's eyes as you try to explain their investment options. Getting people to really understand is a challenge. One that T. Rowe Price has been meeting ever since 401(k) plans came into existence. We realize that the more people know about their plan and their investment options, the more likely they are to make sound decisions. That's why T. Rowe Price offers a full range of communications programs—from seminars and videos to newsletters and retirement planning software. We understand that some of your employees are sophisticated investors and others are novices, so we tailor our programs to help people at both ends of the spectrum and everyone in between. In many cases, your employees' future financial security will be riding on how wisely they invest their 401(k) money. The more they know, the better their chances are. If you'd like to learn about how we can help your employees become more confident investors, please call John R. Rockwell at (410) 581-5900.

Invest With Confidence

T. Rowe Price

CHAPTER TWO

ELIGIBILITY

 22 What is "vesting"?
"Vesting" refers to the ownership of a retirement plan benefit. Participants' 401(k) contributions—adjusted for investment gains and losses—are fully vested from day one. However, participants are not necessarily vested in, or entitled to, their employer's contributions right away, even though the money has been put into their individual accounts.

 23 When is the company contribution vested?
Plan sponsors have some flexibility in deciding vesting schedules when they set up the plan. Typically, employer contributions are fully vested when the participant reaches age 65, dies or becomes disabled. All plans must fully vest participants if the plan is terminated for any reason, regardless of their number of years of service or if a large number of participants (generally, more than 20% of the work force) are let go at one time.

Some plans fully vest participants immediately; others don't vest them at all until they have five years of service, and still others phase in vesting, gradually increasing the portion of employer contributions the participant owns. By law, participants must be fully vested in their employer's contributions after seven years of service.

 Below are four sample vesting schedules that satisfy legal requirements. Schedules 1 and 2 represent the minimum legal requirements. Schedule 1 requires 100% vesting after five years; Schedule 2 requires 100% vesting after seven years.

Most 401(k) plan sponsors follow Schedules 2, 3, or 4, each of which vests at a rate of 20% per year of service.

Years of Service	1 % Vested	2 % Vested	3 % Vested	4 % Vested
		Sample Vesting Schedules		
0	0	0	0	0
1	0	0	0	20
2	0	0	20	40
3	0	20	40	60
4	0	40	60	80
5	100	60	80	100
6	100	80	100	100
7	100	100	100	100

24 **How long do I have to wait before I can participate in the 401(k) plan?**

Most companies require new employees to complete one year of service before they are eligible to participate. Employee turnover is usually highest during the first year of employment. By requiring a year of service, companies avoid added administrative costs; this also excludes temporary and other short-term employees who aren't likely to participate in the plan anyway. The waiting period also helps companies pass various non-discrimination tests.

25 **Why can't I join the plan until I reach age 21?**

Employers are legally permitted to exclude employees under the age of 21 and those companies with a high percentage of young employees usually do. Statistically, most employees under 21 don't participate in their company 401(k) plans and their lower participation rates hurt highly compensated employee (HCE)/non-HCE ratios and reduce the amount other employees may contribute to the plan.

26 **How are my years of service determined?**

Employers have a choice of two legally acceptable methods to determine an employee's years of service: hours of service or elapsed time.

The *hours of service* method credits participants with one year of service for every 1,000 hours worked within a given 12-month period. This method lets an employee earn a year of service in less than a 12-month period. When determining the first year of service, the employer must start the calculation from the date of employment; otherwise, any 12-month period may be used. Most plan sponsors, in fact, shift to the plan year date because it's too cumbersome to track hours of service according to each employee's anniversary date.

With the *elapsed time* method, years of service are determined by counting each 12-month period from the employee's date of employment to the date of termination, regardless of how many hours the employee worked. For example, employees hired on October 23 receive credit for a year of service on each October 23 they are still employed.

Both methods are widely used, some in tandem at many companies. The hours of service method is often used to determine employee eligibility and the elapsed time method to determine vesting. If you use hours of service to determine employee eligibility, you must also use the hire date as the starting date for the calculation.

☞ **NOTE:** *The calculation rules for the hours of service method are fairly complicated. Both methods involve complex regulations for determining breaks in service and rights upon re-employment.*

27 **What happens to my 401(k) account if my company re-hires me?**

With today's mobile work force, many employers re-hire previous employees. Prior years of service must be counted if the re-hired employee had earned a vested benefit—if the employee has contributed even one dollar to the 401(k) plan—during his or her previous period of employment with the company. (Remember, employee contributions are always vested.)

In other instances, the length of the employee's prior period of employment and the length of the gap between employment periods determine vesting. *Generally, prior service must be counted if the gap between employment periods is less than the greater number of full years the employee worked during his or her first term, or five full years.*

In order to retain credit for prior service, re-hired employees may be required to re-establish their accounts by returning any prior distributions to the plan. Any employer contributions they may have forfeited—if they left before being fully vested—must be re-deposited to their accounts. This doesn't happen often but it could, especially if your company offers a dollar-for-dollar match.

28 **My company has many business units, each with its own benefit plan. Employees of some units have 401(k) plans and some do not. What happens if I am transferred?**

Employers are required to count all years of employment for benefit eligibility and vesting purposes, regardless of how many business units an employee has worked in.

When employees are transferred from a business unit that has a 401(k) plan to one that does not, they will no longer be able to make contributions. But because the employees are still legally active for the same employer or group of employers, their account balances cannot be distributed. The participant accounts must therefore be frozen, with future adjustments only for a full share of investment gains and losses. If employees transfer from one unit to another before being fully vested, their years of service in the new unit count toward vesting the frozen account.

THE Leading Source in the
  401(k)/Pension Market for
  Research-Based
  Marketing Services

ARI

ACCESS RESEARCH, INC.

8 Griffin Road North • Windsor, Connecticut 06095
203-688-8821 • Fax 203-688-2053

Plan Sponsors

Employee Satisfaction Studies
Communications Strategies
Investment Attitude and
  Behavior Research

Service Providers

Product Development Support
Market Entry Plans
Distribution Strategies
Productivity Analysis
Training and Enrollment
  Programs

CHAPTER THREE

TAXES

What are the tax advantages of participating in a 401(k)?

Investing in a 401(k) offers participants an important tax advantage. Money employees contribute is subtracted from their gross pay before Federal income taxes are withheld—employee contributions are not reported on their W-2s—so each dollar is fully invested in the plan. A 401(k) plan is a tremendous boost to savings when you consider that an employee in the 28% tax bracket, for example, earns only 72 cents for every $1 dollar after Federal taxes alone are deducted. Savings can be realized on state taxes, as well.

Employee Carl Cashman earns $50,000 a year and contributes $5,000 a year to his 401(k) plan. That contribution reduces his taxable income to $45,000. Assuming he's in the 28% bracket, he saves $1,400 in Federal income tax (28% of $5,000).[2] $5,000 is invested and working for Carl in the plan, but his take home pay declines by only $3,600, or even less if state income tax is a factor.

Another big advantage is tax-deferred growth. Appreciation or earnings on Carl's 401(k) contributions are not taxed until he withdraws money from the plan. Moreover, although his 401(k) savings are eventually taxed (except the after-tax contribution portion), he could be in a lower tax bracket at retirement.

Why does the government provide these tax advantages?

To help your employees accumulate as much money as possible for retirement. Taxes are a major impediment to personal savings. Generally 25 cents to 35 cents of every employee dollar earned is paid in taxes. Uncle Sam permits tax-favored savings in plans such as 401(k)s because without them it would be difficult if not impossible for most people to save what they need for retirement, especially with the impact of inflation. The government is willing to forego current tax revenue to reduce the very real risk that millions of Americans might

---

[2] Remember, there is a limit to the Government's benevolence. As discussed in Question 1, the IRS sets a cap on annual pre-tax contributions. For 1995, it is $9,240.

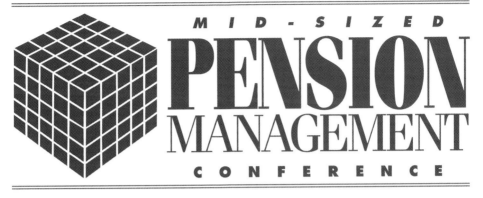

MID-SIZED PENSION MANAGEMENT CONFERENCE

OCTOBER 15-18, 1995
Palmer House Hilton, Chicago, IL

An educational and peer networking conference for companies with pension, profit sharing, 401(k) and retirement savings plans with assets of $1 million or more.

Featuring more than 70 workshops on such key issues as:

Participant investment education and communication
Fiduciary risk
ERISA-mandated regulations

Plan design and administration
Selecting service providers
Monitoring and evaluating the plan

Partial Listing of Sponsors

Aetna Investment Services, Inc.
CIGNA Retirement and Investment Services
Fidelity Investments
Godwins Booke & Dickenson

Investment Advisers, Inc.
John Hancock Funds
Merrill Lynch
NYL Benefit Services Co.
The Northern Trust Company

Prudential Defined Contribution Services
Scudder, Stevens & Clark, Inc.
State Street Bank and Trust Co.
Wachovia Trust Services

Other programs in the Mid-Sized Pension Management Conference series include:
San Francisco – February 25-28, 1996
New York – June 2-5, 1996

For information contact the Conference Coordinator at
(919) 541-9339 • Fax (919) 541-9026

KENAN-FLAGLER
BUSINESS SCHOOL
UNC-CHAPEL HILL

Organized by:
PHOENIX-HECHT

wind up without enough money to live comfortably in retirement—a burden that, ultimately, might pose a bigger threat to public coffers.

 Why is it a real risk that many may not have adequate retirement savings? What about Social Security?

You must explain to your employees that Social Security was never intended to be the sole source of retirement income. It was conceived as one leg of the "three-legged stool;" the others are private sector pension plans and personal savings. Today, the average male Social Security recipient collects $760 per month and the average female recipient receives $580 per month—hardly princely sums.

More to the point, Social Security is grappling with serious problems that no one could have anticipated when it was enacted in 1935. The most obvious is that people live a lot longer today than they did then. In 1930, the average American life expectancy was 59.7 years. In 1989, it was 75.3 years—an additional 16 years in which to collect Social Security benefits. Today, the average Social Security recipient collects more in benefit dollars than he or she ever paid into the system, even when investment earnings on contributed funds are considered.

In other words, current Social Security benefits are funded by taxes paid by today's workers. Given demographic trends, that's a serious problem. In 1950, there were 16 people in the work force for every one retiree collecting Social Security; today, there are only three workers for each beneficiary, and by 2030, it is projected that the ratio will be a startling two to one. This suggests a greater tax burden on a narrower tax base. Since Social Security is controlled by our political system, its benefits can be lowered or redefined as demographic changes cause political shifts.

The bottom line is that no matter how loudly politicians swear that Social Security benefits are sacred, soon there simply won't be any choice but to make some major changes. Congress will have to reduce Social Security benefits by increasing taxes (for current workers and/or for all but the least affluent benefit recipients) or by redefining the eligibility rules—or both. This explains why the government wants to encourage and facilitate individual efforts to save for retirement, *and why it's critically important for your employees' future security that they do so.*

Do I pay any taxes on the amount I contribute to my 401(k) plan?

Employees' pre-tax contributions, by definition, go into the plan before Federal income taxes are withheld. Federal taxes are due later, when the money is taken out of the plan. Employees are required by law to pay Social Security tax on all contribution amounts, pre- and after-tax. However, once they reach the maximum Social Security wage ceiling of $61,200, no further Social Security taxes for the retirement, survivors and disability portion of Medicare—now 6.2% of wages—is due; only the remaining Medicare portion—1.45% of wages—is deducted from their contributions for that year.

All states except Pennsylvania exempt 401(k) contributions from state income tax. Some municipalities tax 401(k) contributions.

Check with your company's payroll processor regarding applicable 401(k) taxes in your jurisdiction.

TIP: If your state or local taxes apply to 401(k)s, advise plan participants periodically, or whenever you distribute other tax information.

33 **Are my Social Security benefits reduced if I have contributed to a 401(k) plan?**

Not necessarily, although distributions from participants' 401(k) accounts could make a portion of their, or their families', Social Security benefits subject to Federal income tax—especially if there are other significant sources of income.

Generally, any other income received by employees in retirement, or when they are disabled, or received by their families after their death—including taxable interest or dividends from personal savings and investment assets, and non-taxable interest from municipal bonds or tax-exempt money market funds—may, if the amount is large enough, make a portion of the participants', or their families', Social Security benefits subject to Federal income taxes.

 TIP: If employees are concerned that their retirement savings distributions will cause a reduction in their Social Security benefits, they should consult with a qualified tax advisor, attorney or CPA.

34 **Since income tax rates may be higher in the future, won't I be better off paying my taxes now and saving outside the plan?**

Employees can't build savings strategies around future tax rates. No one can predict future tax rates, or how much taxable income they will have after retiring. Although it is possible that the amount an employee contributes to the plan today will be taxed at a higher rate when it is withdrawn, it seems likely that the unique savings advantages of the 401(k) will more than offset any future tax increases.

Although the money isn't as accessible in a 401(k) as it is in a standard savings account, the painless automatic payroll deduction for a 401(k) contribution takes the planning and discipline out of saving. The company match is free money and employees who don't participate literally throw dollars away. Even without a company match, the amount of money employees can accumulate over time on a tax-deferred basis is likely to be substantially greater than any amount they could accumulate outside the plan—even after plan withdrawal taxes. Finally, it is likely that the average employee's tax bracket will be lower in retirement.

If the company matches employee contributions, and participants are fully vested in the matching contributions when they withdraw the money, they should wind up with more money by saving in the 401(k) plan, even after taking the 10% early withdrawal penalty.

In general, it is more sensible to do short-term, after-tax saving outside the 401(k) plan. The 401(k) is, first and foremost, a retirement savings plan and, considering the alternatives, *it is imprudent to use it as a short-term savings vehicle.*

35 **Why must I pay a penalty tax if I take my money out of the plan before age 59½?**

The government is willing to pass up much-needed tax revenues today to help employees save for retirement, but isn't willing to subsidize personal expenditures. The penalty tax is meant to discourage employees from withdrawing the money early.

 How is the 10% penalty tax calculated?

This tax applies to the entire untaxed amount that is distributed prematurely to the participant—regardless of whether the participant is still employed by your company. Thus, a 48-year-old participant who receives a $10,000 distribution would pay a $1,000 penalty tax in addition to Federal income tax on that amount.

NOTE: *Distributions after early retirement at age 55 and after the participant ceases to be an employee are not subject to this tax penalty. Other exceptions include distributions taken:*   *1. for catastrophic, unreimbursed medical expenses;*
2. after the participant is disabled or dead;
3. for certain annuity distributions at any age.

 If I leave my company, how can I avoid paying taxes on the account balance in my 401(k)?

Employees can't avoid paying taxes, but there are three ways they can delay doing so. The first way is to leave the money in the former employer's plan if the vested account balance is at least $3,500 and the participant is younger than the retirement age specified in the plan. The second way is for the employee to transfer the account balance to a defined contribution plan offered by the new employer, although this may not be permitted until after the employee satisfies the new plan's eligibility waiting period. The third, and probably most popular option, is to transfer the money into an IRA rollover account. If the employee's plan has all its 401(k) assets invested with one organization such as a mutual fund family, employees should be able to transfer their 401(k) accounts to an IRA rollover without changing funds.

Employees who transfer their 401(k) account balances into an IRA rollover account can transfer their money into another employer plan at a later date. Such a transfer, however, is possible only if the employee deposits and retains the amount from the 401(k) account in a separate IRA account.

Is there any way for an employee who wants to spend all or part of his or her 401(k) account to avoid the mandatory 20% withholding tax?

Employees who request a direct transfer from their 401(k) account to an IRA rollover account may subsequently withdraw all, or a portion, of the amount transferred out of the IRA without having taxes withheld. However, regular income taxes and possible penalty taxes will still have to be paid on this amount.

CHAPTER FOUR

UNDERSTANDING 401(k) PLAN INVESTMENTS

39 **How are 401(k) plans structured?**

Most 401(k) plans offer a variety of investment alternatives in which employees can choose to invest. The majority offers a menu of mutual funds; many publicly held companies also offer their employees the option of company stock. There are also commingled trust accounts and insurance company separate accounts which are similar to mutual funds in concept and design but are not available to the retail investor.

A mutual fund is both an investment management company and a type of investment vehicle that pools the money of thousands of investors to buy specific investments. Mutual funds give the average individual investor many of the advantages that historically have been available only to institutional investors and wealthy individuals. Mutual funds come in all shapes and sizes and include a wide variety of stocks and bonds, precious metals, real estate, emerging markets, index funds that replicate broad-based securities indexes, and so on. Most 401(k) plans, however, offer a limited selection of funds—usually three to eight.

Employees need to understand that when they invest in a mutual fund, their money buys shares of that fund. The price of each fund share is called its "net asset value" or NAV. The NAV of their shares rises and falls depending on what happens to the mutual fund's investments. If they own shares in a stock fund, for example, and its investments rise in value, so does the price or value of their shares.

As mutual fund shareholders, they get a proportionate slice of the fund's profits and losses on its investments, and a proportionate piece of any dividends the fund's investments may pay. If they invest in a mutual fund outside a 401(k), they can opt to take their dividends in cash. This is not possible in a 401(k) plan because withdrawals from the plan are strictly limited by law. (See Question 16.) Any dividends earned by a mutual fund investment in their 401(k) plans are automatically reinvested in more fund shares.

The mutual fund investor also benefits from a professional portfolio manager and research staff, much greater diversification (see Question 57), and volume discounted transaction costs. The fees a mutual fund pays to buy and sell shares are much lower than those the individual investor pays for a similar investment through a broker. Assuming equal performance, the lower the fee, the bigger the return on investment.

40 **Typically, what type of investment funds are offered in 401(k) plans?**
The types of funds most commonly offered in 401(k) plans are:

➤ Money market fund

➤ Guaranteed Investment Contract or (GIC) fund

➤ Government bond fund

➤ Corporate bond fund (Income fund)

➤ Growth and income fund (Common stock fund)

➤ Growth fund

➤ Aggressive growth fund

➤ Balanced fund

➤ Index fund

➤ International fund

➤ Emerging markets fund

➤ Lifestyle fund (Asset allocation fund)

➤ Company stock fund

Employers aren't required to offer any specific investment options, but those who comply with the Department of Labor's ERISA Section 404(c) regulations must offer at least three types of funds having a range of asset classes and risk levels. Although compliance is voluntary, many employers comply because they perceive that it will increase their protection from any liability suits brought by participants who are dissatisfied with their investment results. (See Question 41.)

41 **Is there a minimum number of investment options my company is required to offer in the 401(k) plan?**
401(k) plan sponsors are not required to offer any specific number of investment options.

In 1993 the Department of Labor issued voluntary guidelines regarding participant-directed defined contribution plans, chiefly 401(k)s.[3] For those who choose to comply, Section 404(c) of ERISA stipulates that plan sponsors must offer their employees *a minimum of three distinct investment options.* In exchange, the Department of Labor shields the plan sponsor from any future liability stemming from participants' investment losses. By "distinct" the government means investments with notably different risk and reward characteristics, such as a money market

---

[3] For a an extensive discussion of Section 404(c) regulations, including a dialogue among 401(k) sponsors and legal experts, see "A Special 404(c) Report," pages 69-79, **A Wing and A Prayer: Defined Contribution Plans and the Pursuit of 24 Karat Golden Years,** Investors Press, 1994.

fund, a growth fund and a bond fund. Whether or not they follow 404(c) guidelines, most employers do offer at least three funds.

As participant account balances—and comfort levels—grow, companies tend to add funds to the investment menu. This reflects the growing awareness among both employers and employees of the importance of maintaining sufficient investment diversification. For participants who have large account balances, many advisors believe it's a good idea to allocate their money among five or six funds for adequate diversification. Even the money in smaller accounts should be diversified to reduce overall investment risk.

There is a limit, however, to the number of investment choices that makes good common sense. Most employers are reluctant to confuse participants by offering more than eight or nine investment choices, and many industry experts concur.

42 **Who selects the investment manager(s) for my company's 401(k) plan?**
As the plan sponsor, your company is responsible for selecting the investment manager(s) who will invest 401(k) contributions. It is also responsible for monitoring manager performance.

ERISA dictates that investment manager or fund selection must be based solely on the "best interests" of the plan participants. Assuming a manager or a fund has a good investment track record, there are other key factors that play into the selection decision: management fees and ancillary services such as communications or educational materials, to name just two. The plan sponsor is also ultimately responsible for ensuring that contributions are invested in accordance with all the legal requirements of a 401(k) plan. (See "Service Provider Selection," pages 38-41.)

43 **How should I invest my money?**
This question opens a Pandora's box: every time you've heard it, you've probably also been warned not to give investment advice. Doing so might someday invite a breach of fiduciary duty lawsuit under ERISA.

No doubt you are committed to giving employees all the tools you possibly can to help them make informed investment decisions. But providing your employees with the information they need without giving investment advice can indeed be a delicate balancing act.

The main reason to give participants investment options and the opportunity to contribute money personally to the plan *is to shift responsibility* for investment results from plan sponsor to plan participant. Legally, you could retain this responsibility by making the investment decisions for all 401(k) assets; however, collectively managing plan assets would be risky, given your participants' diverse objectives.

Generally, your answer to the question of how to invest should be "no comment." Be confident that your duty is to equip participants with the means to answer the question themselves. How aggressive plan sponsors should be about educating their participants is another hotly debated matter. (See "Employee Communication," pages 22-30.) Brochures, newsletters, videos, seminars, workbooks and software simulations are among the most popular and useful tools.

44 **Can I decide how to invest all the money in my account, including employer contributions?**

Most 401(k) plans permit employees to choose how their own contributions are invested, but some do not allow employees to direct the investment of employer matching or profit-sharing contributions. Typically, employers may retain investment control of their contributions when:

➤ Employer matching contributions are in the form of company stock.

➤ The contributions are part of profit-sharing arrangements, or are intended to replace a discontinued defined benefit plan.

➤ Employer contributions are not yet vested (the participant hasn't been employed long enough by the company).

45 **How do I know the right amount is being credited to my 401(k) account?**

Some participants relegate their account statements to a bottom drawer and forget about them. Many others, however, check each one closely. Unfortunately, many of the methods participants use to analyze their statements lead to incorrect conclusions.

Participants in daily valued plans have less concern that their accounts are being credited properly because valuation methods are more precise and understandable. With other valuation methods, however, certain assumptions used to allocate investment income are important to know, particularly when participants use computers or calculators to analyze their statements.

Typical assumptions used in allocating investment income are:

➤ All deposits and withdrawals occurred at the mid-point of the valuation cycle.

➤ The investment return for the valuation period occurred in uniform increments each day of the valuation period.

➤ Company stock acquired during the valuation cycle is priced by taking the average purchase price for that period.

 TIP: Periodically, you might distribute a guide to the account statement which not only shows how to read it, but explains how investment returns are computed.

46 **How do I know how well my investments are doing?**

At least once a year participants receive 401(k) financial statements that show the amounts they've contributed and how their investments have performed. Some plans report on a quarterly or monthly basis. For information on mutual funds, you might refer participants to other information sources such as business newspapers and magazines.

47 **Is the principal invested in my account protected against loss?**

The answer is an emphatic "no."

Inform your participants that there isn't *any* investment, inside or outside your 401(k) plan, that is absolutely guaranteed against complete loss. Even the Federal Deposit Insurance Corporation (FDIC) isn't totally fail-safe; it's designed to protect deposits in the event of isolated bank failures during generally

Help.

Mention retirement and what springs to mind? Fishing? You wish.
Try working. Today, people are living longer, healthier lives. Which is wonderful,
provided they have the means to enjoy it. Which brings us to CIGNA.
As one of the nation's leading managers of 401(k) and pension funds, backed
by $34 billion in assets, we build retirement plans that work.
So our customers won't have to. Call 1.800.997.6633.

CIGNA Retirement &
Investment Services

normal economic and business conditions. How far it would go toward protecting deposits in a major economic collapse is anyone's guess. Similarly, the most conservative fund offered by your plan could be wiped out by such a broad-based collapse.

As for "Guaranteed Investment Contracts" (GICs)—they are insurance company investment vehicles (insurance company IOUs), and *are not* insured or guaranteed by the government.

One of the most important lessons your investment education program should teach participants is to recognize the inherent risk in each investment option. *Above all, the term "no risk" should never be used to describe any plan option.*

48 How often can I change my 401(k) plan investment allocation?

Employers complying with the ERISA 404(c) regulations must enable participants to transfer money among the plan's investment funds *at least quarterly*. If the plan offers a fund that is considered a volatile investment—company stock, for example—more frequent transfers must be allowed. The regulations don't dictate the frequency; it must be commensurate with the fund's level of volatility.

Employers decide when and how often participants will be allowed to transfer funds based on:

➤ the administrative costs of operating the plan under a given valuation frequency;

➤ the capability of the recordkeeper to handle investment changes;

➤ concern about participants making bad investment decisions by attempting to time the market.

Each time participants move money from one fund to another, the current value of their accounts must be calculated. With "traditional" recordkeeping systems, the more frequent the valuation, the more expensive the plan. Until recently, most plans featured either monthly, quarterly or semi-annual valuation.

During the past few years there has been a widespread shift to the more cutting-edge daily valuation systems. Since account balances are updated every day, transfers are possible on any trading day. Keep in mind, however, that not all plans with daily valuation permit daily transfers—that way employers can discourage participants from abandoning long-term strategies for short-term "market timing".

 NOTE: *Transfer and valuation processes commonly confuse participants. It's essential that your communications explain in detail how your plan's investment transfer process works. Be sure to indicate exactly when the transfer will be made. (See "Employee Communication," page 26.)*

49 How often should I change my investment allocation?

The mantra for plan participants is this: *let your long-term retirement income goals guide every investment decision you make for your 401(k) plan.* To accomplish this, participants should review and fine-tune their asset allocation every year or two to reflect their long-range goals. Significant life changes that alter the participant's investor profile—marriage or divorce, children or educational needs, for example—and substantial asset growth are the big justifications for changing asset allocation.

One of the most difficult temptations in investing, even for the pros, is to pull out of an investment during a big market drop. *Participants should be warned not to overreact to either good or bad news*; the results can be equally damaging. Participants who resisted the overwhelming urge to bail out after the 1987 stock market crash not only recovered their losses but ended up achieving respectable gains. At the other extreme, participants who respond to big gains in the market indices by shifting larger amounts than they normally would allocate into stocks are prone to panic attacks when major drops occur. There is only a handful of legendary market timers—the rest of us should not play with fire!

What can I do if I don't like my plan's investment options?

Despite the often painstaking efforts of plan sponsors, not all participants like their plan options. Although it is important to give employees opportunities to voice their complaints, you simply cannot conceive a plan tailored to meet the collective needs of every one of your participants. Employees have the choice to stop participating or never to start, but you want to make obvious your effort to offer a plan that meets diverse needs.

 SMART PILL: Rather than wait for feedback, why not actively solicit it? Survey your employees periodically, or hold focus groups, to see how well your participants understand your plan's investment options.

Survey information provides valuable insights that participation percentages alone cannot. You may find that more education about the present options, not more funds, is what participants really need—and want. Remember: in terms of favorable employee perception relative to employer cost, the 401(k) plan is one of the most cost-effective benefit plans.

What information must my employer provide to me?

By law, not much, but that is only because ERISA was passed at a time when retirement benefits were almost universally employer-funded. The most common plan was a defined benefit pension plan, for which the company took full charge of funding and investing plan assets.

Today, many employers offer 401(k) plans as their primary or sole retirement program; the writers of ERISA did not anticipate this shift to participant-directed defined contribution plans. Now good or bad investment performance translates directly into a higher or lower retirement benefit, yet most people lack sufficient knowledge and understanding of retirement planning and investment principles. Moreover, most employees have a large, and increasing share, of the ultimate responsibility for ensuring their own financially secure retirement. The lesson is clear: *information is critical.*

Your employees are legally entitled to receive a Summary Plan Description, Summary Annual Report and an Annual Statement. They may not necessarily be entitled to a copy of the prospectus for each mutual fund they invest in, although they must get the prospectus for your company stock fund if it is part of the 401(k) plan.

Many plan sponsors recognize the huge gap between what employees need (and want) and what the law requires. Whether or not they comply with the 404(c) regulatory guidelines, most plan sponsors provide additional investment information and educational support to help their employees invest for their retirement.

52 Help! I want to learn about the funds I've invested in, but these mutual fund prospectuses are Greek to me. What are the key points I should look for?

The prospectus is a legal document required by the Securities and Exchange Commission; written by lawyers, it is no wonder it makes for extremely dull and often unintelligible reading. Fortunately, you can find the most valuable information in the first few pages.

Participants should look first for the fund's *investment objectives*. What is the fund's investment goal and what basic investment strategy will the fund manager use to reach that goal? In a growth and income fund, for example, the primary objective might be capital appreciation (growth of principal), with income as a secondary objective. In a government bond fund, on the other hand, the investment objective might be current income and safety of principal.

The description of a stock fund's *investment strategy* should indicate whether the portfolio manager is a value investor (one who looks for stocks selling cheaply relative to their true value) or a growth investor (one who concentrates on stocks expected to enjoy rapid earnings growth). Will the fund try to time the market? If the portfolio manager believes the stock market is going into a decline, for example, will he switch out of stocks and into money market instruments in an attempt to minimize the fund's losses? Or does the manager intend to stay fully invested at all times, riding out the market's ups and downs?

In the prospectus section on *investment objectives*, participants will also find a description of what the fund intends to invest in.

EXAMPLE

Here's an excerpt from the prospectus of a small-cap fund: *"The fund normally invests at least 65% of its assets in common stocks of small and medium-size companies in the early stages of their life cycle. It may invest up to 20% of its assets in foreign securities."*

Advise participants to look for the fund's *fees and operating expenses*. The most important number here is the *expense ratio*: the fund's annual operating expenses expressed as a percentage of its total assets. The lower the ratio, the lower the fund's expenses. In 1993, for example, actively managed stock funds had an average expense ratio of 1.43%; the lowest-cost stock index fund, by contrast, had an expense ratio of just 0.19%. If, on average, two mutual funds have the same investment performance, the fund with the *lower expense ratio* will have the higher return. *It's net returns that matter*.

Finally, look at the fund's *performance history*. This shows how well, or how poorly, this mutual fund has performed over time. It will also indicate what its portfolio turnover rate has been: how frequently the portfolio manager has sold assets and bought new ones. According to John Rekenthaler, Editor of *Morningstar Mutual Funds*, in 1994 the average fund turned over 88% of its holdings.

The more aggressively the fund trades investments, the higher its trading expenses. But a high turnover rate is not necessarily bad; it should be considered in the context of the participant's individual investment goals and the fund's long-term total return.

Be sure participants compare the fund's past performance and portfolio turnover rate only with those of funds with similar objectives. Often, a prospectus will suggest an appropriate benchmark to use in judging only a particular fund's performance. A growth fund or a growth and income fund might use the Standard & Poor's 500 Index as a benchmark, for example. A small-cap stock fund might use the Russell 2000 Index.

WHAT TO LOOK FOR IN A MUTUAL FUND PROSPECTUS
Investment options
Investment strategy
The expense ratio: fees and operating expenses
Performance history

 How can I get more information about the funds I've invested in?
Deciding what and how much information to provide for participants can be difficult, since their needs are so different. Some plan sponsors deal with this problem by providing basic information to all participants and by making additional resources available for those who may be interested.

If your participants are willing to do a bit of research on their own, a great education is within easy reach. There are research services that provide mutual fund data, as well as popular personal finance magazines, a variety of newsletters, associations—the list literally goes on and on.[4]

 SMART PILL: Consider creating a list of outside educational sources as a general handout or as a feature in your newsletters.

---

[4] See Annotated Bibliography for suggested educational resources easily accessible to 401(k) participants.

INVESTMENT TERMINOLOGY

The following definitions are generally accepted, however individual plans and investment managers may have slightly different interpretations.

54 **What is risk tolerance?**

"Risk tolerance" refers to an investor's comfort with the risk inherent in a given type of investment. It is often called the "sleep factor"—the level of risk an investor can handle and still be able to sleep peacefully. An investor who buys volatile stocks but is afraid of losing money and would likely bail out at the first downturn in the market has a low risk tolerance. No one should invest beyond his or her risk tolerance zone, and plan sponsors should be vigilant against any service providers who pressure 401(k) participants into doing so. Your goal is to educate participants about key investment concepts so that they are comfortable extending their risk tolerance when it serves their ultimate investment goals.

SMART PILL: Consider distributing risk tolerance worksheets periodically to help your participants understand their attitudes toward risk.

55 **What is asset allocation?**

How assets are divvied up among various asset classes, or types of investments, is known as "asset allocation." In the 401(k) context, asset allocation refers to the way in which participants split their accounts among the plan's different investment options. According to some experts, asset allocation is the single most significant influence on investment return: as much as 94% of a portfolio's performance can be attributed to long-term asset allocation versus security selection or investment timing.[5]

This means that risk-averse participants who play it safe by putting all their money in the most conservative fund—a short-term government bond fund, for

---

[5] Gary P. Brinson, L. Randolph Hood, and Gilbert L. Beebower, "Determinants of Portfolio Performance," *Financial Analyst's Journal*, July-August, 1986, p. 39.

example—will be limited to a very narrow, and perhaps lower, range of invest-ment results. More important, this conservative approach may actually undermine well-intentioned savings efforts, since fixed-income investments are most vulnera-ble to the erosion caused by inflation. *Investing too "conservatively" actually creates a different kind of risk, and one that is just as damaging: "retirement risk," or* the risk of not accumulating enough money to achieve an adequate level of retire-ment income.

Plan participants who invest only in fixed-income instruments can raise their potential long-term investment return by 25% or more simply by changing their asset allocation to include a modest 10% in equity investments.

56   What does re-balancing mean?

Different funds appreciate at different rates. Over time, asset classes with a higher rate of growth will make up a larger percentage of the total mix than the participant originally intended. Re-balancing transfers money from faster-growing investment funds to slower-growing funds in order to maintain a pre-determined asset allocation mix. *An imbalance in the original allocation not only alters the return expectations, it changes participants' risk exposure, too.*

Suppose a participant's target asset allocation is 50% in a growth fund and 50% in a principal stable fund. The equity fund is expected to grow faster over the long term, cre-ating a substantial imbalance after several years. By not rebalancing, the participant is exposed to a much greater potential loss if stock prices drop. Many experts say that participants should transfer a portion of the excess in their equity account to the principal stable fund regularly.

57   What is diversification?

Diversification is the strategy of spreading your assets among a number of investments. Used in tandem with asset allocation, proper

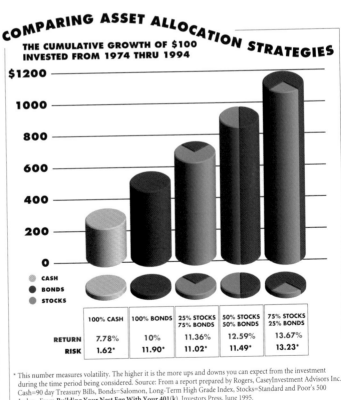

COMPARING ASSET ALLOCATION STRATEGIES

THE CUMULATIVE GROWTH OF $100 INVESTED FROM 1974 THRU 1994

	100% CASH	100% BONDS	25% STOCKS 75% BONDS	50% STOCKS 50% BONDS	75% STOCKS 25% BONDS
RETURN	7.78%	10%	11.36%	12.59%	13.67%
RISK	1.62*	11.90*	11.02*	11.49*	13.23*

* This number measures volatility. The higher it is the more ups and downs you can expect from the investment during the time period being considered. Source: From a report prepared by Rogers, CaseyInvestment Advisors Inc. Cash=90 day Treasury Bills, Bonds=Salomon, Long-Term High Grade Index, Stocks=Standard and Poor's 500 Index. From **Building Your Nest Egg With Your 401(k)**, Investors Press, June 1995.

diversification enables investors to establish a risk and return equilibrium suited to their individual temperaments and retirement needs.

Investors who put all their investment eggs in one basket simply make themselves too vulnerable to loss. *This approach may make sense for speculators, but not for retirement plan investors.* As an example: many experts feel participants should think hard about investing more than 10% to 15% of their total 401(k) contributions in company stock funds or GIC funds. (See Question 58.) No matter how "hot" an investment your own company may appear to be, it's simply too risky for your participants to commit more than that modest percentage of their retirement savings to the fortunes of their employer.

According to the precepts of Modern Portfolio Theory, the foundation of modern investing, the more widely investors diversify, the lower their risk. A well-diversified portfolio smoothes out the high and low returns of various types of investments over the long haul. This applies equally to individual or mutual fund portfolios. Diversification is the major tool defined benefit plan sponsors use to protect plan assets from the downside of specific markets (e.g., international equities) or investment management styles (e.g., growth investing).

In 401(k) plans, where the responsibility for employee retirement asset investment decisions shifts to participants—and their account balances continue to grow—participants must strive to maintain a proportionate degree of diversification. It is important that they put this principle into practice: that's a major reason why plan sponsors continue to add new fund choices.

58 What is a GIC fund?

A GIC, *or guaranteed investment contract*, is a short-term loan to an insurance company made by investors, in this case 401(k) participants. In exchange, the insurance company guarantees participants a fixed interest rate, paid on a timely basis for the term of the loan (typically one to five years) and the repayment of principal at the end of the contract term.

A GIC is very much like a certificate of deposit (CD) except that it's offered by an insurance company instead of a bank. Unlike a CD, in which both principal and interest are "guaranteed" by the Federal Deposit Insurance Corp., a GIC is "guaranteed" only by its issuing insurance company and applicable state insurance fund.

If a GIC issuer fails, holders of its contracts may be forced to accept a lower interest rate than they were promised, and may have to wait longer than expected to recoup their principal. In fact, they may never get all their money back. While this doesn't happen often, since 1991 three reputable insurers that sold GICs have faltered or failed financially and were taken over by regulatory authorities, resulting in investor losses.

A *GIC fund* is a pool of GICs issued by different insurers. This fund is potentially safer than a GIC issued by only one insurer because it offers greater diversification: if the pool buys GICs from 15 to 20 different insurers and one of them fails, the impact to the investor won't be nearly as great. A certain percentage of the pooled fund's assets will mature and be reinvested every year. The pool may pay a fixed rate for a year at a time, or it may change its rate more frequently as it buys new contracts.

A GIC fund is the most common type of "principal stable fund," so named because the value of the investor's principal stays constant instead of fluctuating, as it would in a stock or bond fund. The investment is maintained at book, rather than market, value.

The main advantage of a GIC fund is stability of principal. The risk of losing the participant's original investment is low because the term of the loan is so short. But this feature is also its disadvantage because the participant's original investment doesn't grow enough to withstand the ravages of inflation.

Plan participants find GIC funds, or principal stable funds, very attractive because the principal amount they invest does not fluctuate in value and the interest rate is fairly predictable. Although this may be a peace-of-mind advantage, participants must understand that it isn't really a savings advantage. A 401(k) investment should meet investment goals—and personal needs—that are, typically, many years away; a GIC's pre-determined interest rate is guaranteed only for a short term. History shows that the investor with a goal ten years or more into the future is likely to earn a better return with a mix of stock and bond investments than with cash equivalent investments like GICs. (See Chart on page 88, to see different asset allocation results over time.)

From a risk standpoint, GIC funds are comparable to money market funds. On average, they beat money market fund returns by about 1% on a long-term basis. One important drawback: GIC funds usually contain restrictive investment transfer and withdrawal provisions. (See Question 60.) Be sure to explain these drawbacks carefully to participants.

SMART PILL: If you offer a GIC or GIC fund in your 401(k) plan, it's wise to advise participants of the credit ratings of issuing insurers; they are available from rating agencies such as Standard & Poor's Corporation, Moody's Investor Service and Duff & Phelps Corporation.

59 What is a money market fund?

A money market fund invests in short-term, high-quality debt obligations (IOUs) such as Treasury bills, bank certificates of deposit, repurchase agreements and commercial paper.[6] It's one of the lowest-risk funds a 401(k) plan can offer. Money market funds deliver long-term returns purely in the form of interest earned, usually in the 4% to 5% range.

Participants earn a fluctuating interest rate in a money market fund because the fund is constantly buying and selling these loans. But their original investment, or principal, remains stable. Their investment in the fund is converted into shares with a fixed value of $1 each (unlike a stock or a bond fund, in which their investment is converted into shares whose price fluctuates depending on how well or poorly the fund's investments perform).

A money market fund is a good place to park money for participants who are nearing a distribution, or are undecided about where to invest.

The main advantage of a money market fund is that the participant's principal is stable. A money market fund doesn't offer a fixed interest rate, like a GIC; its fluctuating interest rate can be an advantage or a disadvantage depending on

---

[6] A repurchase agreement is a contract in which a seller (usually of U.S. government debt) agrees to repurchase securities from the buyer at an agreed upon price and time. A common "repo" involves a securities dealer who borrows from an investor (typically a corporation with excess cash) to finance its inventory, using securities as collateral. Commercial paper is the very short-term loans of corporations with excellent credit ratings.

which way interest rates move.

A participant's money is more diversified in a money market fund than in a GIC fund because the participant is lending to a wide range of corporate borrowers, as well as to the Federal government. In a GIC fund, participants lend to borrowers within only one industry—the insurance industry.

The main disadvantage of a money market fund is that participants' principal doesn't grow. It's very vulnerable to inflation, just as it is in a GIC fund. *History shows that after inflation and taxes (which are due once participants withdraw money from their 401(k) plan account) a money market fund investment like Treasury bills barely grows at all over periods of ten years or more.*

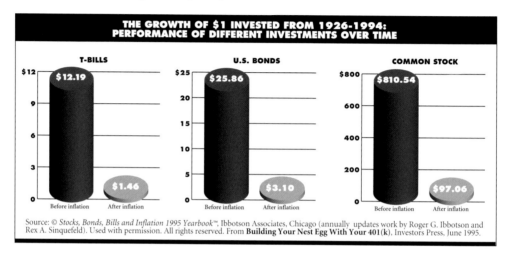

THE GROWTH OF $1 INVESTED FROM 1926-1994:
PERFORMANCE OF DIFFERENT INVESTMENTS OVER TIME

Are money market funds risky? Not very during normal economic conditions although, theoretically, they could be risky if a business backing the fund fails. That failure would lower the overall interest return of the fund, and possibly even result in loss of principal. Some money market funds use derivatives, which increase risk, as well.

60 Why can't I transfer money from the GIC fund to the money market fund?
If participants were permitted to switch between the two types of funds GIC fund issuers would have to sell investments at a loss. It is only by prohibiting transfers from the GIC fund to a money market or similar fund that GIC issuers protect themselves from such exposure.

Historically, GIC funds have been backed by the assets of one or more insurance companies. These assets are invested in long-term, fixed-income investments which, as a rule, return more interest than the rate the insurer guarantees the GIC fund holder. Therein lies the insurer's profit—and its ability to offer your plan an investment with stability of principal and a relatively consistent rate of return.

Money market funds, on the other hand, are backed by short-term investments. As a result, the interest they earn fluctuates more rapidly than that of a GIC fund. (Remember, the GIC fund's interest rate changes only when any of its component contracts expire and are reinvested.) While the long-term return of a GIC fund is greater than that of a money market fund, there will be periods when money market funds will yield a higher investment return, possibly by as much as 2% to 3%.

61   What is a bond (or income) fund?

A bond fund, or income fund, invests in the debt obligations of large U.S. corporations. A short-term bond fund buys bonds that have an average maturity of less than three years; an intermediate-term fund buys bonds that have an average maturity of three to ten years; and a long-term fund buys bonds with an average maturity of ten years or longer.

Each bond within the fund earns a fixed amount of interest; the collective interest of all the bonds in the fund make up the fund's overall interest rate. But the fund's interest rate doesn't stay fixed; it fluctuates constantly as the fund buys and sells bonds (a mutual fund doesn't hold bonds to maturity).

The value of an investor's principal also fluctuates. When interest rates fall, shares in a bond fund increase in value because existing bonds pay a higher rate than new issues. Fund shares drop in value when interest rates rise because newly issued loans pay a higher rate than do old loans. The risk that your principal will shrink because of rising interest rates is called "interest rate risk." All bonds carry interest rate risk.

The total return from any bond fund, corporate or government, is the interest earned plus or minus any changes in the value of investors' principal, as reflected in the market price of fund shares.

The longer the maturity of a bond, the more value it will gain if interest rates fall, and the more value it will lose if interest rates rise. Long-term bond funds are much more volatile than short-to-intermediate bond funds because they react more dramatically to changes in interest rates.

Other factors beside interest rates affect the value of a bond's principal. If the credit rating of the issuing company declines, or if the company files for bankruptcy protection, its value will drop. Any event affecting an individual bond will have an impact on the fund.

You can't judge a bond fund's performance by its yield alone; as junk bond investors discovered when interest rates rose in 1989 and 1990, a bond fund can pay a very high yield, but at the same time produce a terrible total return. The result: investors receive handsome interest payments while their principal steadily dwindles in value.

Always look at a bond fund's total return—the yield, plus or minus any changes in the value of your principal, as reflected in the market price of your fund shares. The term "income fund" can be misleading to participants, since it suggests a stable value. Be sure you explain what it really means.

62   What are the advantages of a bond fund?

A short-to-intermediate term bond fund provides a steady stream of income as it keeps participants' capital fairly safe. These funds tend to be less volatile than stock funds, so keeping part of their 401(k) money in a bond fund can help participants lower the volatility of their portfolios. Money invested in a bond fund is liquid and can be moved to another fund without any transfer restrictions typical of fixed-rate investments, such as principal stable or GIC funds.

A long-term bond fund provides a relatively high stream of income, and has a potentially high total return if interest rates fall. But a long-term bond fund carries a high risk of loss to principal: if interest rates rise, the value of participants' shares could plummet.

63 What are the disadvantages of a bond fund?

The main disadvantage of bond funds is that *they expose participants to interest rate risk.* All too often, participants don't realize that they've assumed this risk. They incorrectly assume that their principal will be stable in a bond fund the way it is in a money market fund or in a GIC fund.

 Bond funds also have a major disadvantage as a long-term investment: historically, they haven't provided enough growth to stand up well to inflation. (See Chart, page 88.) Inflation, of course, is the biggest enemy of a fixed-income portfolio, since over the long term it erodes returns. That's why, important as safety of principal is, it may actually be risky for participants to put all their 401(k) assets in bond funds. This doesn't mean that bonds have no place in a portfolio that's invested for a long-term goal; it's always a good idea to diversify your long-term investments. There have been decades—from 1928 to 1937, for example—when the bond market outperformed the stock market.

64 What is a government bond fund?

A government bond fund buys IOUs issued by the U.S. government and/or its agencies, such as the Government National Mortgage Association (known as "Ginnie Mae"). The Federal government issues three basic types of IOUs: Treasury bills, which mature in one year or less; Treasury notes, which mature in one to ten years; and Treasury bonds, which mature in ten years or longer.

The interest on government obligations is typically lower than the interest paid on corporate bonds of similar maturities because there's virtually no risk that the Federal government and its agencies will default on their loans. Unlike corporations, the government can always raise money by imposing or increasing taxes. Although there's no default risk, government bonds or government bond funds are not necessarily risk-free.

 If a participant buys an 8% government bond and holds it to maturity, he or she would receive a fixed 8% yield for the life of the bond. But the interest received as an investor in a government bond fund isn't actually fixed because a mutual fund doesn't hold bonds to maturity. The fund constantly buys and sells bonds; the interest earned by fund shareholders fluctuates.

As with a corporate bond fund, the value of the investor's principal in a government bond fund doesn't remain fixed, either. It rises and falls as interest rates change. Again, if the prevailing interest rate goes up, the value of investors' principal—and the net asset value price (NAV) of their fund shares—goes down. Who would pay full price for a $1,000 bond that pays 7% when newly issued $1,000 bonds pay 8%?

NOTE: *Government funds that invest in short-term obligations will experience little or no fluctuation in market value. Of course, the longer the term of the bond, the greater the interest rate risk.*

Besides Ginnie Mae bonds, other government agency bonds found in government bond funds include "Freddie Macs" (issued by the Federal Home Loan Mortgage Corp.) and "Fannie Maes" (issued by the Federal National Mortgage Association).

Invest in North America's Future

DIVERSIFY

Employees are learning the importance of diversification in pursuing their investment goals for a secure retirement. The NAFTA Advantage Fund, the newest Harris Insight Fund, offers a unique opportunity to distinguish your company's 401(k) fund selection.

The NAFTA Advantage Fund invests in securities of issuers in Canada, Mexico, and the United States that the advisers believe will benefit from the North American Free Trade Agreement.

The Investment Adviser, Harris Investment Management, Inc., with more than $13 billion under management, has combined with its northern and southern neighbors, Bank of Montreal Investment Counsel Limited and Bancomer Asesora de Fondos, S.A. de C.V., respectively. This team creates a unique three-way professional investment management alliance uniformly focused on seeking to identify and invest in favorable situations throughout North America.

To make the Harris Insight NAFTA Advantage Fund or other Harris Insight Funds a part of your company's Defined Contribution Plan, call a Harris Investment Representative at (800) 982-8782.

Ginnie Maes, Fannie Maes and Freddie Macs are mortgage-backed bonds. The stream of income they pay investors comes from homeowners' mortgage payments. There's little risk of default on these bonds because the Federal government has guaranteed repayment of the mortgage loans backing them. But mortgage-backed bonds have unique "prepayment risks." For example, officially these bonds have 30-year maturities, but in reality a 30-year mortgage is generally repaid in seven years when, typically, houses are refinanced or sold. This prepayment risk makes mortgage-backed bonds particularly vulnerable to interest rate changes. Like all bonds, mortgage-backed bonds lose value when interest rates rise. But unlike other bonds, they also lose value when interest rates fall significantly.

When interest rates fall by several percentage points, millions of homeowners rush to refinance; they pay off the mortgages backing Ginnie Maes and other mortgage-backed bonds, and they take out new loans at the prevailing lower interest rate. As a result, the investors in Ginnie Mae bonds get their principal back much sooner than they expected, and must reinvest it at the much lower prevailing rate. The investor's real return in any mortgage-backed investment, like Ginnie Maes, depends on how fast homeowners pay off the underlying mortgages. That, in turn, depends on many unpredictable variables including interest rates, the housing market and the job market.

On the plus side, to compensate investors for prepayment risk, Ginnie Maes and other mortgage-backed bonds usually yield somewhat more than other government bonds.

65 What is a growth and income fund?

Growth and income funds invest in blue-chip stocks, the common stocks of established U.S. companies with a history of steadily growing earnings and reliable dividends.

Growth and income funds are a good investment for relatively conservative investors who want long-term growth. In a rising stock market they won't grow as rapidly as growth funds, but in a falling stock market they don't lose as much value, partly because blue-chip dividends offset some of the decline in the stock prices.

66 What is a growth fund?

A growth fund is a mutual fund that invests in the stocks of companies whose earnings the portfolio manager thinks will grow faster than average. The main goal of a growth fund is to achieve long-term growth of principal, not to earn current income for its investors.

The differences among growth funds reflect individual portfolio manager investment "styles" as well as their predictions about growth prospects for a whole industry sector or specific stocks. A manager who has a "top-down" style, for example, looks for attractive industry sectors and then finds promising individual stocks that are undervalued in comparison to the rest of the market. A "bottom-up" manager looks for attractive companies across industry sectors.

Historically, growth funds have produced a higher long-term return than growth and income funds. Over the long term, the stocks of growing companies are likely to grow at a faster rate than inflation. If that happens, the real buying power of 401(k) participant money will grow faster than inflation, as well.

On the downside, growth funds are vulnerable to short-term market fluctuations. Over periods of ten years or longer, the stock market has always increased in value. But in any two or three-year period, the price of stocks can seesaw for many reasons.

Therefore, a growth fund may not be a good investment for participants who will need their money in a year or two, and have to cash out when their fund shares might have dropped in value. Participants who invest in a growth fund should be patient and comfortable with a long-term perspective.

67 What is an aggressive growth fund?

An aggressive growth fund, sometimes called a "capital appreciation" or "small-cap" fund, invests in the common stocks of small emerging companies. The objective for these funds is to get the most growth for the investor through less conservative strategies.

The investment return for aggressive growth funds comes chiefly from increases or decreases in the value of fund stocks since little, if any, dividends are paid by emerging companies. These corporate managers want to plow everything back into the company to achieve the highest possible level of growth.

Aggressive growth funds are among the most volatile mutual funds. In a rising stock market, they may outperform the average stock fund. In a falling stock market, however, they'll lose more value than the average stock fund. Aggressive growth funds require long-term investment stamina.

68 What is a balanced fund?

Investors in a balanced fund decide to pay a portfolio manager to divide their money between stock and bond investments. The portfolio manager's freedom to allocate the fund's total assets depends on the individual fund's provisions. (The fund prospectus will indicate how much leeway the portfolio manager has been given.) The portfolio manager actively buys and sells securities to improve the fund's return, derived from a combination of interest and dividend income along with increases and decreases in the value of the securities.

A balanced fund provides investors with both income and growth. It's a compromise: in a rising stock market, a balanced fund won't earn as high a total return as a pure stock fund will. But in a falling stock market, a balanced fund won't lose as much as a pure stock fund; its interest and dividend income will cushion the fall. When interest rates fall, balanced funds do well because falling interest rates are good for both bond and stock prices. However, when interest rates rise, the value of both stocks and bonds is likely to fall.

69 What is an index fund?

An index fund invests in all the stocks or bonds that make up a particular market index. Investment decisions are managed by a computer instead of a human being.

The S&P 500 Index, for example, consists of the top 500 companies (banks, utilities, corporations) with the greatest market value of stock outstanding in the U.S. The performance of these 500 stocks is a benchmark for the stock market's overall performance. An S&P 500 Index fund buys the 500 stocks that make up

the index. Other major indexes are the Russell 2000, which tracks the performance of the stocks of 2,000 medium to small companies; the Shearson Lehman Brothers Government/Corporate Bond Index, which tracks the performance of investment grade bonds (those with good-to-excellent credit ratings) and the Dow Jones Industrial Average, which tracks the performance of 30 blue-chip stocks.

An index fund investor can expect to earn the average return, and suffer the average losses, of the particular market that index replicates. By contrast, an investor in an actively managed fund expects the portfolio manager to pick investments that outperform the market as a whole.

Historically, however, only about a third of actively managed funds have achieved this goal. Some investors question the value of active portfolio management.

An index fund has lower operating expenses than an actively managed fund. Shareholders aren't paying for a star portfolio manager or a big research staff. In addition, because an index fund simply buys and holds one group of stocks (or bonds), its trading expenses are minimal. Lower costs translate into a higher return for shareholders.

Is there a downside to index funds? Remember that some actively managed funds do outperform the market, sometimes by a substantial margin. An index fund, by definition never will, in good markets or bad. In a falling stock market, the index fund will fall, too; a talented or lucky investment manager can minimize the losses of an actively managed fund in a down market by changing its portfolio mix and buying and selling the right assets at the right time.

What is an international fund?

70

An international fund invests in the stocks and/or bonds of non-U.S. companies. (401(k) plans usually offer stock funds.) International funds should not be confused with global funds, which can invest in the securities of any country, including the U.S.

Why should plan participants consider an international fund? One simple reason is opportunity. Our economy is truly international; today, the U.S. stock markets represent only about one-third of the world's publicly traded stocks, down from two-thirds a mere 20 years ago. By limiting themselves only to U.S. stocks, participants are ignoring two-thirds of the investment opportunities in the world. Some of those investment opportunities are in economies that are growing more rapidly than the mature U.S. economy.

Another advantage of owning international stocks is portfolio diversification. Foreign stock markets don't correlate (move up and down in tandem) with the U.S. stock market. A good performance by international investments can help cushion a portfolio at a time when the U.S. market is falling.

One important disadvantage of international investments is their added layer of risk. Not only are returns affected by the changing values of stocks, they are also affected by shifts in monetary exchange rates. Before the fund can buy shares on a foreign exchange, the investment amount must be converted into the local currency; after selling shares, the amount must be converted to dollars. Like all risks, currency risk works both ways: if the U.S. dollar declines in value compared to other currencies, the investor's shares in an international fund can increase in value. But if the dollar rises in value relative to other currencies, the price of his or her fund shares can drop.

71 What is an emerging markets fund?

An emerging markets fund is an international fund that invests in Third World or developing countries such as Indonesia, Malaysia, the Philippines, Peru, Colombia, Argentina and the former Eastern-bloc countries. Some of these economies are growing at the rate of 15% or more a year—much faster than the mature U.S. economy, which in healthy times grows at about 3% a year. An emerging markets fund gives investors the opportunity to profit from rapid growth.

The enormous potential demand for goods and services in developing nations can make many companies and their shareholders very rich. Just think of all those millions of people in the former Iron Curtain countries who are eager to buy disposable razors, breakfast cereal, life insurance, automobiles and countless other products an American consumer takes for granted.

Let caution prevail, however: the road from communism or totalitarianism to a free market economy is far from smooth as anyone reading headlines about the former Soviet Union can testify. Emerging markets are vulnerable to economic and political crises (Mexico is a good example), and investors should expect more volatility in an emerging markets investment than in a domestic fund or an international fund that invests in the world's developed nations.

72 What is a lifestyle (asset allocation) fund?

A lifestyle or asset allocation fund invests in several types of assets—U.S. and foreign stocks, bonds, real estate company stocks, money market instruments—that plan participants could normally buy in individual funds. These funds provide diversification that weathers most market or economic conditions over a participant's lifetime. Often, a 401(k) plan will offer several asset allocation funds, each with a different investment mix, ranging from conservative to aggressive.

Some asset allocation funds keep a fixed percentage of total assets in each type of investment. Others give the portfolio manager freedom to change the mix, emphasizing investments that will perform best in the current environment. These funds provide an alternative for plan participants who do not want the burden of making investment decisions for their 401(k) accounts.

73 What is a company stock fund and should I invest my money in it?

Some publicly traded companies give their 401(k) matching contribution in company stock rather than in cash. Many plan sponsors also offer their stock as a 401(k) investment option. Participants have the advantage of knowing more about their employer—its strengths, weaknesses and future prospects for growth—than they do about any other company.

But no matter how impressive the company or rosy its prospects, it's a risky business for participants to have both their current income and retirement nest egg riding on the success of a single company. Skeptics should consider the volatility of IBM's stock: between mid-1992 and mid-1993, Big Blue's stock price fell from $100 a share to just over $41, recovering in 1995 when it reached $75.

Most investment professionals recommend investing no more than 10% to 15% of total assets in any one stock. Participants in 401(k) plans ought to be well diversified before increasing their investment in company stock beyond 15%.

 What are the tax advantages of receiving company stock?

Under present law, only the tax on appreciation (not on the initial acquisition cost) in a participant's 401(k) plan account's holding of company stock is deferred until the participant sells the stock, even if distribution shares are not rolled over to an IRA.

However, if the participant rolls the stock into an IRA, this special tax treatment is lost when the participant withdraws money from the IRA. If the shares are rolled into an IRA and then sold, capital gains taxes may or may not apply to the participant.

 Participant Lucky Larry Largecap invests in 1,000 shares of company stock which have an average purchase price of $20. At the time the stock is distributed to Larry it has a market value of $35 a share. If Larry takes a distribution of the shares and does not roll them into an IRA, he must pay tax at that time on only $20,000. It's not until he sells the stock that he'll have to pay tax on the additional $15,000, and then capital gains rates will apply.

CHAPTER SIX

GETTING 401(k) MONEY BEFORE RETIREMENT

 75 It's my money! Why can't I take it out whenever I want?
True, 401(k) contributions belong to participants, but since participants haven't paid Federal income tax on the money, Uncle Sam can impose whatever access restrictions he wants. The government is willing to postpone current tax revenues to encourage employees to save for retirement, but restricted access and tax penalties for early withdrawals are the trade-offs.

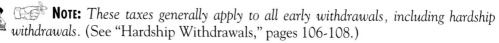 **76 If I withdraw money from my account before I retire, what is my tax penalty?**
The entire amount that participants withdraw is subject to Federal income tax. If participants are active employees and under the age of 59½, generally they will have to pay a 10% penalty tax. Withdrawals may also be subject to state and local income taxes and, in some states, similar "premature distribution" tax penalties, as well.

 NOTE: *These taxes generally apply to all early withdrawals, including hardship withdrawals.* (See "Hardship Withdrawals," pages 106-108.)

77 If I stop contributing, can I take my money out of the plan at any time?
No. It's a common misconception among employees that they can take out their money if they stop contributing. Withdrawals are permitted only for the reasons that have been approved by the government. (See Question 16.)

78 Can I withdraw money to buy a second home?
No. Withdrawals are permitted only to buy a primary residence, and the participant must meet hardship withdrawal requirements. (See Question 16.)

 79 Can I take money out of the plan for reasons other than a hardship withdrawal?
Check your plan.
Legally, the vested portion of participants' accounts may be distributed anytime after they leave your company, regardless of the reason. Typically, distributions are made for the following events:

> death   > retirement after age 55

> disability   > termination of employment

> lay-off   > termination of the plan (if there is not a successor plan).

When you're here,

your mind shouldn't be here.

At AUL, we believe the best thing we can offer pension plan sponsors is one less thing to worry about. That's why we offer top quality customer service coupled with sophisticated cutting edge products that are uniquely geared to meet your and your employees' needs. The result—a retirement savings product that relieves you of the day-to-day hassles so you aren't worrying about them while you're away from the office.

We offer multiple investment options from industry leaders such as Fidelity Investments® and Twentieth Century.

Our interactive voice response system, AUL TeleServe, allows participants to track their investments and move money between options on a daily basis.

And, we've created a powerful multi-media program that our retirement plan specialists use in enrollment meetings as well as for ongoing participant education.

Make your next 401(k) vendor selection your best, and your last. For more information on AUL's Defined Contribution 401(k) products, call Brian Sweeney, Vice President of Pension Marketing, today at (317) 263-1161.

American United Life Insurance Company®
Indianapolis, Indiana

The 401(k) Specialists

CHAPTER SEVEN

LOANS

 80 **Can I borrow money from my 401(k) account?**

Check your plan.

Most employers allow plan participants to borrow from their 401(k) accounts, although they aren't required to do so.

Legally, loans can be allowed for any reason. Most plans, however, permit them only for specific, approved purposes such as buying a house or paying college tuition. Employers have two good reasons for restricting plan loans: (1) loans add to the cost of administering the plan; and (2) loans can defeat the main purpose of a 401(k) plan, which is to ensure that your participants retire with an adequate nest egg.

For most participants, loans are usually preferable to withdrawals. All plan participants automatically qualify for loans; unlike borrowing from a bank, there are generally no credit standards to meet. A 401(k) loan also earns money because participants pay the interest to themselves on the borrowed amount.

 81 **Are there any drawbacks to taking a loan from my account?**

Yes, and they can be significant, depending on the participant's circumstances.

Usually, participants who leave a job must pay any outstanding balance on their loans in order to achieve a tax-deferred rollover to an IRA. If they don't, the IRS treats any remaining loan balance as an early withdrawal on which they owe income taxes and a tax penalty. If they've spent all the money, they could be in a tough spot.

Some employers allow participants to continue to make scheduled payments after they leave the company; but most accelerate the payments of any loan balance. In any event, the loan balance must be paid off if the separated participant takes a distribution.

If participants have the added burden of paying off a loan, they may not have enough money to contribute to their 401(k) plan. If they stop making contributions, they lose the benefit of the company match and defeat the long-term goal of the plan: to save for retirement.

How much of my total account can I borrow?
Check your plan.
　　Most plans stipulate a maximum of 50% of the participant's vested account balance, up to the legal maximum of $50,000. Some plans set a minimum loan amount, usually between $500 and $1,000.

 Do I need my spouse's agreement in order to borrow from my 401(k)?
　　Possibly. Some plans follow joint-and-survivor rules, which means that participants and their spouses must have the option to receive the retirement payout in the form of lifetime annuity payments. If your plan follows these rules, spouses may have to sign off on participant loans. Some plans require spousal consent to a loan even though it may not be subject to the joint-and-survivor rules.

　　Requiring a spouse's signature also prevents a participant from borrowing against the assets in the 401(k) plan while a Qualified Domestic Relations Order (QDRO) is pending. (See "QDROs" pages 48-49.)

 What are the repayment requirements for a 401(k) loan?
　　All loans must be repaid through a series of equal payments. Typically these payments are automatically deducted from the employee's paycheck. The entire amount must be repaid within five years with one exception: if the loan is used to buy a principal residence, some plans grant the participant 25 years to repay it.

How long will it take to get my loan check?
　　The time it takes to get a loan varies widely among plans, depending on administrative procedures. In some plans, participants initiate a loan through a voice response system and the check is sent one or two days later. Other plans send the participant an application which must be reviewed by a plan representative and meet the plan's loan requirements. The representative then requisitions a check for the loan amount. Any additional time involved will depend upon the plan's check processing procedures. Most plans batch benefit-related checks every day, or once a quarter.

 SMART PILL: Be sure your employees know exactly how much time to allow for loan processing so they can plan accordingly.

Where does the money I borrow come from?
　　The money participants borrow comes from their 401(k) accounts. Some plans tell participants which fund they must borrow from; others automatically take a proportionate amount from each investment in the participant's account. Most plans, however, let the participant choose.

How is my loan accounted for?
　　A 401(k) loan is treated much like a bank loan; the borrowed amount is considered an asset even though it is no longer in the participant's account.

Jessica Jones has $17,000 in her 401(k) account, with $11,000 invested in a principal stable fund and $6,000 in a growth fund. Assume she wants to borrow $5,000, and decides to take it from the principal stable fund. Her account would still have a $17,000 balance, with $6,000 remaining in the principal stable fund, $6,000 untouched in the growth fund and $5,000 accounted for as an asset—now as a loan.

The Impact of Jessica's Loan on Her 401(k) Account		
Fund	Before Loan	After Loan
Principal stable	$11,000	$ 6,000
Growth	6,000	6,000
Loan	0	5,000
Total	$17,000	$17,000

 If my 401(k) money is invested in several funds, which one should I borrow from?

That decision depends on various factors, not the least of which is the loan's impact on asset allocation.

Participant loans are fixed-rate investments. To maintain the current asset mix, participants should probably borrow the money from a fixed-rate fund. Why? The only return the loan will generate is its interest, unlike an equity fund, which could generate higher returns through capital appreciation and dividend payments. If participants borrow from their growth fund, for example, their original asset allocation strategy shifts.

 SMART PILL: Withdrawing loan money from a fund with similar return characteristics—another fixed-income fund—maintains their asset allocation.

 What is the cost of a loan and why do I have to pay a fee to borrow my own money?

Loans take time to process; they add a significant administrative expense to the plan, so many plan sponsors charge loan origination and annual administrative fees based on recordkeeper charges for loan processing and administration.

 How is my loan interest rate determined?

The interest rate on a 401(k) loan must be comparable to the rate an unrelated third party would charge for a similar loan. Beyond that, it's up to the employer to set its own loan interest rate. Most plan sponsors base their rates on the prime rate (the interest rate banks charge their best corporate customers), adding another one or two percentage points. If the prime rate is 7%, typically the interest rate on a 401(k) plan loan is 8%. With some plans the interest rate is fixed for the loan term; other plans charge a variable rate and adjust it periodically.

 Is the interest I pay on my loan tax-deductible?

Generally. The IRS considers a 401(k) loan a tax-deferred investment. The government's view is that the money would have been invested in one of the other funds had it not been borrowed. Moreover, Uncle Sam isn't willing to accept a reduction in future tax revenue just because plan participants borrow money. A tax deduction on the interest participants pay themselves would be akin to a tax break on top of a tax break.

This rule applies even if the participant borrows the money to buy a house. Interest on home equity loans is deductible only when the home is the only collateral the borrower offers.

With a 401(k) loan, the account balance is generally used as the collateral, thereby disqualifying the interest deduction. The interest might be deductible if:

1. the loan is taken from a source other than the participant's own pre-tax contribution, and

2. the loan is secured solely by the mortgage on the participant's residence, or

3. the loan proceeds are used to purchase an income-producing investment outside the plan and the "investment interest" rates apply.

Few plans use the participant's residence as collateral because of the paperwork involved. Participants should consult their own tax advisor about applicable tax issues related to loans.

 92 Who receives the interest I pay on my loan?
The procedure for applying loan interest repayments varies among plans. Most, however, credit payments to participant accounts so that one participant loan does not affect the investment returns of all participants.

A few plans establish a collective participant loan fund which in effect "owns" all outstanding participant loans. Here, the interest a participant pays on a loan is credited to the loan fund. The plan sponsor calculates a blended return from this loan fund and gives each participant with a loan a proportionate share of the interest the fund earns.

 93 How are my loan payments reinvested?
Check your plan.
Most plans handle loan payments as if they were new contributions. If a participant's new contributions were split equally between two funds, for example, the loan repayments would be split between these funds.

Plans which create collective loan funds generally hold participant loan payments—principal and interest—in the loan fund until the loans have been fully repaid. Participants can then distribute the repaid loan among their other investment funds.

 94 What happens to my loan·if I leave my company?
This is one of the tougher issues to handle—both for employees and plan sponsors—regardless of why or when employees leave.

Obviously, a loan can no longer be repaid through automatic payroll deductions. (See Question 81.) There are a few possible scenarios:

Mary Moremoney decides to leave her company. She has an unpaid loan balance of $4,000 and is eligible for a $10,000 benefit distribution. The neatest solution would be for her to repay the loan balance and then transfer the entire $10,000 to an IRA rollover account to avoid paying any taxes. That presumes that Mary has $4,000 available just for this purpose.

If Mary elects to take a distribution instead, her entire $10,000 will be subject to the 20% mandatory withholding tax applicable to distributions. (See "401(k) Distributions," pages 111-116.) After deducting the loan balance and taxes she would end up with only $4,000, and she will probably have more taxes to pay since the 20% mandatory withholding tax will not, in all likelihood, cover her full tax liability.

If Mary took the $4,000 distribution and then changed her mind and decided she wanted to do a 100% tax-deferred rollover to an IRA, she would have to come up with an additional $6,000 to deposit to her IRA. (IRAs are not permitted to hold 401(k) loans, so participants can't escape the tax liability through an IRA rollover.)

These tax and cash flow problems could be avoided if Mary transferred her entire account balance, including the loan balance, to her new employer's 401(k) plan. Unfortunately, most plans have a one-year waiting period which rules out this possibility. Even for those plans that grant immediate eligibility, plan-to-plan transfers create an additional administrative expense, and a transfer involving a loan balance adds another level of complexity. Few plan sponsors want to touch such a transfer.

 NOTE: *What it comes down to is that most participants in these circumstances are forced to consider the loan as a taxable distribution. That means they must pay tax on money that was already received and spent.*

95 What happens to my loan if I'm laid off?
Loan payments must still be made, even if participants are not working. If participants stop making loan payments, the company may have to report the unpaid balance as a tax distribution. If the layoff is only temporary, a distribution may not be possible, however, since the participant is still considered an employee.

SMART PILL: Given the huge potential tax hit facing a laid-off employee with an outstanding loan, it's a good idea to advise all participants about these possibilities periodically, and *whenever* they plan to take a 401(k) loan. It's impossible for anyone to predict their future employment situation, so participants should be reminded that a 401(k) loan has its own special risk.

96 Can I use my 401(k) account as collateral for a bank loan?
No. 401(k) accounts are protected from creditors under Federal bankruptcy law. (See Question 121.) However, participants' 401(k) balances probably enhance their credibility with potential lenders.

We've helped
shape over 4,000
401(k) plans.
Each one
specially crafted.
No two alike.

It's crystal clear why so many choose Kemper. We create a 401(k) with the flexibility to help achieve long-range goals and address the specific needs of your company. For a bundled plan, Kemper Preferred K™ offers turnkey administration. Or we'll help you create a customized, unbundled plan designed to work with your local third-party administrator. In either case, you're backed by state-of-the-art software and on-line data access.

We're dedicated to a consistent, long-term approach to mutual fund management. Let Kemper help your employees build the tomorrows they dream of today. Call your financial representative or Kemper Mutual Funds, 1-800-621-5027, ext. 7830.

KEMPER MUTUAL FUNDS

We're Building Tomorrows Today℠

CHAPTER

EIGHT

HARDSHIP WITHDRAWALS

97 If I need money before I retire, under what circumstances can I make cash withdrawals as an active employee?

By law, withdrawals by active employees are permitted only for the following qualified financial hardship reasons:

> ➤ paying college tuition for the participant or a dependent

> ➤ buying a primary residence

> ➤ covering un-reimbursed medical expenses

> ➤ preventing a foreclosure or eviction from a primary residence

There are other financial hardships, but most employers play it safe and follow the Treasury Department's guidelines rather than risk the wrath of the IRS.

Keep in mind that if your plan allows after-tax contributions, these legal restrictions do not apply. After-tax contributions can usually be withdrawn for any reason.

 SMART PILL: When employees join the plan be sure to spell out withdrawal restrictions.

98 How do I prove that I qualify for a hardship withdrawal?

Participants over age 59½ need not prove anything; in most cases they can make withdrawals without penalty. All other employees must meet the IRS hardship withdrawal requirements. (See Question 16.) The Treasury Department gives two alternative ways to demonstrate financial hardship: the *"certification"* and the *"suspension"* methods.

Using the certification method, participants must provide relevant financial information and sign a form stating that funds are not available from any other source. The suspension method requires participants to suspend contributions for at least one year. Some employers pick one of these methods, while others let participants choose between the two. Offering both methods not only meets the various needs of all your participants, but can actually benefit the plan.

Participant Susie Stock, age 25, is scraping together the money to buy her first home. It is easy for her to prove she has no other source of money, so the certification method is her best option; it enables her to continue contributing to the plan. That's a real advantage to the plan sponsor: since Susie is a non-highly compensated employee (non-HCE), her ongoing contributions help the plan pass the non-discrimination tests.

 On the other hand, Ben Bond, an HCE, is applying for a hardship withdrawal to finance his move from a $350,000 home to a $1 million home. He certainly can't provide financial information to show other funds are not available, so the suspension method is a better option for him.

☞ **NOTE:** *If your 401(k) plan allows loans, participants are required to borrow the maximum available amount before they qualify for a hardship withdrawal, regardless of which qualification method(s) your plan uses.*

99 My company laid me off; can I get a regular distribution or a hardship withdrawal?

It depends on whether the layoff is temporary or permanent. If the layoff is temporary, the employer may treat the employee as if he or she had not actually separated from service. A withdrawal may be permitted if the employee has a legitimate financial emergency. A permanent layoff is the same as termination, in which case the participant is eligible for an outright benefit distribution.

100 How much can I withdraw from my account for a financial hardship?

Legally there is no dollar limit on participant withdrawals for financial hardships; plans can set their own restrictions, however. If a participant needs $10,000 to cover the initial costs of buying a home, he or she should withdraw enough money to cover the tax that must be paid on the withdrawn amount.

101 Are my employer's contributions included in the amount I'm eligible to withdraw for a financial hardship?

Check your plan.

Many plans permit participants to withdraw only their contributions, adjusted for investment gains and losses. Some plans also permit participants to withdraw vested employer contributions in the event of financial hardship. Plans that do not allow employer contributions to be withdrawn are designed that way to safeguard the money from being used for any reason other than retirement savings.

102 What taxes will I owe on a hardship withdrawal?

Participants owe ordinary income taxes on everything except amounts they originally contributed to the plan on an after-tax basis. They'll also owe a 10% early withdrawal tax penalty if the withdrawal occurs before age 59½. Many people assume incorrectly that if they meet the IRS definition of financial hardship, they won't owe the 10% penalty. (See Question 76.)

Of all the places people
choose for their retirement, this
is one of the most popular.

As one of the nation's largest institutional investment managers, there isn't a more desirable place for your company's 401(k) plan than

The Prudential. Fifty million Americans already know and trust us for their financial and employee benefit services, which goes a long way toward

With more than $188 billion in assets under management, The Prudential is one of the nation's largest investment managers.

increasing employee participation in your retirement plan. Of course, employee acceptance alone doesn't account for our $30 billion in defined contribution assets. That took time; we're in our fourth decade as a DC manager.

It took investment experience, as exemplified by our institutional investment managers, such as Jennison Associates. And it

took innovation

Over 50 million Americans trust The Rock to help them reach their financial goals.

in recordkeeping, like an imaging system that gives service reps on-line access to every piece of correspondence in a participant's file – originals, within seconds. All of which makes the journey

Jennison and other specialty managers offer diversification and institutional investment management expertise.

to retirement smoother for everyone, and

The Prudential a comfortable place to retire indeed. For a free brochure on The Prudential 401(k) plan, contact your Prudential representative or call us toll-free at 1-800-862-3344. The Prudential 401(k)

Prudential Defined Contribution Services

Nancy Nickel, age 42, withdraws $20,000 from her account for a down payment on a house, a qualifying hardship. If her combined Federal, state and local tax rate is 40%, she should earmark $8,000 of her withdrawal for income taxes. Plus, she'll have an additional $2,000 penalty tax. Nancy will wind up with only $10,000 of her $20,000 withdrawal. If she actually needs $20,000 she will have to withdraw twice that amount—$40,000—in order to have the $20,000 she needs after paying all the taxes due.

Participants should consider an early withdrawal from the 401(k) plan only as a last resort: *it's terribly expensive money.*

 SMART PILL: Remind participants that if they take a hardship withdrawal, the company will only withhold 20% of their distribution for taxes. They will owe the rest of the taxes on that distribution when they file their next income tax return. To make sure they have enough to cover the taxes and penalty due the following April 15th, advise them to set the money aside immediately or ask you to withhold more than the customary 20%.

103 **What is the procedure for making a hardship withdrawal?**
Check your plan: each establishes its own administrative procedures.

Usually the participant begins the process by submitting an application form to the plan administrator or other representative. At some companies, participants can request the form through the plan's voice response system. If the request is approved by the plan representative or a review committee, a check is requisitioned and issued.

104 **How long will it take to get my money after I apply for a hardship withdrawal?**
The time varies depending on the hardship withdrawal and your plan's check processing procedures. Many plans batch-process all benefit-related checks to reduce expenses; they can do this as often as daily, or as infrequently as quarterly.

401(k) Distributions

105 **What happens to my 401(k) account when I retire?**

At retirement, participants get all the money in their 401(k) accounts, subject to their plan's vesting schedules. (Employees are fully vested at "normal" retirement age, which can't be later than 65.) But participants face an important decision: what's the best way to take their money? The following choices must be considered—and discussed with a spouse, human resources manager, qualified financial advisor and tax accountant. Not all plans offer every option; in fact, many plans require a retiring participant to take a lump sum distribution.

The Taxable Lump Sum Distribution: Participants can take all their 401(k) money in a lump sum. Unless they transfer this distribution into a rollover IRA, they'll owe income taxes on the whole amount. Under current tax law, however, individuals receiving a lump sum from a 401(k) after age 59½ can sometimes lower the applicable tax rate by using a calculation called "five-year averaging."[7]

The advantage of the lump sum distribution is that in some cases it allows participants to pay lower taxes than they would normally owe, thanks to the five-year averaging tax break. The disadvantage is that after participants have taken the lump sum distribution, their money is, of course, no longer in a tax-deferred retirement account. The only way they can avoid tax on any future earnings is to invest the money in tax-exempt instruments, which tend to be lower-yielding investments.

The Lifetime Annuity: Some plans give participants the option of taking a 401(k) payout in the form of a lifetime annuity, purchased from a private insurance company. An annuity pays a monthly benefit for the participant's lifetime or, in the case of a joint-and-survivor annuity, for the lifetimes of the participant and his or her spouse. An annuity provides a guaranteed lifetime benefit, but because it's a fixed benefit, its purchasing power will be reduced every year by inflation. Also, once the annuitant(s) die(s), there is nothing to pass on to beneficiaries.

---

[7] Refer participants to their tax advisor for an explanation of how using five-year averaging may be beneficial in their particular tax situation. Warn participants about the common misconception that the tax on a distribution can be paid over a five-year period; this is not correct.

YOUR EMPLOYEES MAY
HAVE A FEW QUESTIONS
ABOUT THEIR 401(k) PLAN

WE HAVE MORE THAN 100 ANSWERS

A New Way to Educate Plan Participants

I t's not surprising that plan participants have lots of questions about their 401(k) plan—how it works; what they can expect to withdraw from it, and when; how to make the most sensible investments for their specific needs; whether or not they should even enroll.

As evidence mounts that employees are not investing early enough, wisely enough or simply enough, plan sponsors and administrators have an increasingly urgent obligation to respond by giving their employees a solid basis for making better decisions about their futures.

That's why this new book from Investors Press is so important.

A New Way to Boost Plan Enrollment

Written specifically for plan participants and eligible enrollees, **Building Your Nest Egg With Your 401(k)** gives them the confidence and knowledge they need to manage their 401(k). Exhaustively researched by its distinguished author Lynn Brenner—personal finance columnist for *Newsday*, a Times Mirror publication with more than a million readers, **Nest Egg** draws on Brenner's extensive experience and the results of interviews with more than 100 large and mid-range plan sponsors and administrators. In concise, *easy to understand* language, this important new book answers more than a hundred of the most commonly asked employee questions about

401(k)s. These independent, objective responses will help your employees make more informed judgements about the value of enrolling early, the maximum amount they should save and which investment vehicles will best help them meet their specific needs and expectations. Throughout this handsome book's 160 pages of text, 4-color tables, charts and graphs illustrate and explain key aspects of saving and investing. *Easy to understand,* thorough and entirely relevant to participant's practical needs, **Building Your Nest Egg With Your 401(k)** is also an ideal way for plan sponsors to comply with 404(c) voluntary guidelines and provide the impartial, third-party information participants need as they plan for a secure retirement.

To learn how to offer Nest Egg *to your 401(k) participants or eligible enrollees , please return accompanying card or if you prefer, contact Investors Press at Fax: (203) 868-9733 or Phone: 203-868-6148 ext 95.*

Continued 401(k) Participation: Participants can leave some, or all, of their money in the 401(k) plan. Generally, they must have at least $3,500 vested in their account to do so. This choice makes sense for participants who like the plan's investment options and whose plan rules permit withdrawals frequently enough to meet their needs.

An IRA Rollover: If participants choose an IRA rollover, they can withdraw money as they need it, subject to the IRA minimum distribution rules, and pay income taxes only on the amount they withdraw. This option is the most flexible: participants' money will remain sheltered in a tax-deferred account; they'll have an unlimited choice of investments for that account; and they'll be able to change investments at will.

 When am I legally required to take money out of my 401(k) account?
Participants must begin to withdraw their 401(k) assets by the April 15 following the calendar year during which they attain age 70½, even if they are still employed. *If they don't, they face severe tax penalties.* If your plan designates an earlier age as the normal retirement age, it may require that terminated employees receive their money at that age.

 What happens if I don't take money out of my account at age 70½?
If a participant doesn't withdraw the minimum distribution amount beginning at age 70½, the plan's continued qualification for tax benefits can be jeopardized and the participants will have to pay a 50% tax penalty on the required minimum distribution amount.

 How much do I have to take out at age 70½?
It depends on the participant's life expectancy, and what elections are made prior to the first required distribution. (The IRS provides an actuarial table showing life expectancies.) To determine the minimum distribution, divide the account balance by the number of years remaining in the participant's life expectancy or by the remaining joint life expectancy of the participant and spouse. It's usually worth doing the calculation both ways to see which is more advantageous. It's possible to come up with different mandatory withdrawal amounts depending on whether one life expectancy is used, or two.

Depending on the elections made to this point, the minimum distribution amount may need to be recalculated annually to reflect the participant's current account balance and life expectancy. Participants must pay tax on these mandatory distributions and they are not permitted to roll them over into an IRA.

 Can I continue to contribute to my 401(k) after I reach age 70½?
Yes, if the participant is still working for the employer who sponsors the plan. Even though participants must start to withdraw money from their accounts, they can continue to make contributions.

Does it make sense to continue contributing after age 70½?
Almost always, *if the participant will continue to receive* an employer's matching contribution. If not, it may not make sense.

How long will it take to get the money in my 401(k) account after I retire?
The only legal requirement plan sponsors have is to give participants the money in their 401(k) accounts within 60 days of the end of the plan year during which the employee separates from service after reaching retirement age. Any benefit payment procedures the employer establishes within that guideline are acceptable, as long as they are followed in a uniform and non-discriminatory manner.

Most plans schedule benefit payments around each valuation period. The participant's account must be valued before a distribution is made; this is not a problem for daily valued plans.

 If your plan is on a quarterly valuation schedule and a participant terminates employment on August 17, the distribution can't be processed until after September 30, the next valuation date. Typically, it takes six to eight weeks to complete the valuation, and another one to two weeks to pay the benefit.

 SMART PILL: Spare your participants—especially those approaching retirement—potential headaches by communicating to them clearly the steps involved in a 401(k) distribution, as well as your plan's benefit payment schedule.

 I didn't get my money until two months after December 31 but the amount was based on my account value as of December 31. Why didn't I receive any interest or investment gains during those two months?
This question is always asked when benefit checks are distributed without adjustment for investment income *between the date the account is valued and the date of payment.* This apparent problem is common to all plans that are not valued daily.

Although some participants may lose by this method at the time of the distribution, some may actually gain. Remind them that in the past they benefited every time an employee terminated, since extra investment income is always distributed among all participants in the plan. *Avoiding this misunderstanding is another advantage of daily valuation:* benefit amounts can be calculated precisely on any day including, theoretically, the day the check is cut.

 **Will I get my money back if I leave the company?**
Yes. Participants are entitled to the money they contributed to their 401(k) account because it is always vested. *Remember: it is always adjusted for investment gains or losses.* This means they may end up taking less with them than they put in.

Sally Stock invested $1,000 of her own contribution in the 401(k) plan's growth fund. When she leaves the company, the value of this fund has dropped, making Sally's investment worth only $925. That's all she'll receive.

114 Is it possible for an employee to accumulate too much money in a 401(k) plan?

Although we all know no one can ever be too rich or too thin, Congress believes we can accumulate too much tax-favored money for retirement. The Federal government imposes a 15% penalty tax on what it considers "excessive" tax-sheltered funds: lump sum distributions in excess of $750,000 and annual distributions in excess of $150,000 (adjusted annually for inflation). These limits apply to distributions from the total of all qualified retirement benefits: 401(k)s, IRAs, defined benefit pension plans, profit-sharing plans and so forth, regardless of whether they are paid by the same or different employers. In many cases, however, smart tax planning can help an employee come out ahead even with accumulated retirement savings that exceed threshold amounts.

☞ **NOTE:** The consequences of accumulating excessive amounts of tax-favored retirement savings are important to your company's highly compensated employees (HCEs); it is a complex area of the tax law. *Remind HCEs to consider this in their financial planning, and to remember the Goldilocks rule: employees incur tax penalties if a distribution is too early, too late, too big or too small.*

HOW SECURE IS A 401(k) ACCOUNT?

115 **Does the Federal government guarantee my 401(k) account?**
No. There is no Federal agency like the Pension Benefit Guaranty Corporation (PBGC) that guarantees 401(k) benefits. Nor is there a need for one.

The PBGC was established to guarantee pension benefits for defined benefit pension plans in case accumulated assets aren't sufficient to pay the promised benefits when employees retire.

Because a 401(k) plan is a defined contribution pension benefit, the employer provides a set contribution—or the mechanism that allows employees to make contributions. The only benefit promised to 401(k) participants is the total amount accumulated in their account balances upon retirement, nothing more. This amount is backed by the plan assets—the mutual fund shares—redeemed to the participant at retirement. There isn't any need to have a Federal agency guarantee 401(k) benefits because the retirement benefit will never exceed the market value of the assets in the participant's account.

The value of participant balances at retirement is determined by the amount of their contributions (and any employer matching contributions) and the performance of the investments they choose. Participants could lose money if their investments perform badly. There is no government guarantee to protect participants from investment losses.

A note of reassurance: there is a government agency (the Pension and Welfare Benefits Administration within the U.S. Department of Labor) that has the responsibility to be pension and 401(k) plan "watchdog" and ensure that employers and trustees play by all the rules.

116 **Does my employer guarantee my 401(k) account?**
No. The employer is a fiduciary for the 401(k) plan, and has legal responsibility for supervising participants' money. To protect the financial interests of participants, the employer is obligated to choose reputable and competent plan

trustees, administrators and investment managers and to monitor their performance. If the employer decides to comply with the Department of Labor's 404(c) regulations, plan participants must have at least three distinctly different investment choices, the opportunity to move their money among these investments at least quarterly, and sufficient information to make sensible, informed investment decisions.

The employer cannot, however, protect against any investment losses participants may suffer.

 117 **What happens to my 401(k) account if I'm fired?**

There's no difference between being fired and leaving one's company voluntarily. Generally, if a participant's 401(k) vested account balance is valued at more than $3,500, he or she may leave the money invested in the plan until age 65.

 118 **What happens to my 401(k) account if I'm disabled?**

Most plans fully vest participants who become disabled, although every plan has its own definition of a qualified disability. If employees can no longer work as a result of qualifying disabilities, they are entitled to receive their vested account balance. If your plan lacks a disability provision, or if participants don't satisfy your plan's definition of disabled, their 401(k) will be treated as it would be in a termination.

119 **How do I qualify for disability status?**

For plans with disability provisions, it's up to the plan sponsor to define disability. Most use Social Security or the employer's Long-Term Disability plan standards.

120 **What happens to my 401(k) account if I die?**

Most plans provide for full vesting in the event of death. When participants enroll in the plan they are asked to designate a beneficiary who will receive their 401(k) funds in the event of their death.

 121 **Is my 401(k) account protected from my creditors if I declare bankruptcy?**

Yes. The U.S. Supreme Court ruled in 1992 (Patterson v. Schumate) that retirement assets qualifying under ERISA, which includes virtually all 401(k)s, can't be touched by creditors in a bankruptcy. However, this protection may be lost the moment you take a distribution, even a direct rollover to an IRA, since IRAs may not, depending on state laws and other variables, enjoy the same protection.

Because there are variables, it's a mistake for anyone to file for bankruptcy without finding out how it might specifically affect their accumulated retirement assets. Even in the same state, interpretation of bankruptcy law can vary from one court to another.

SMART PILL: Recommend to participants who are thinking about filing for bankruptcy that they consult a lawyer in their district to find out how local courts treat 401(k) assets.

122 **If I get a divorce, is my spouse entitled to a share of my 401(k) money?**
Probably. The money accumulated in a 401(k) during a participant's marriage is considered a marital asset, and in a divorce would be divided between spouses according to individual circumstances and the laws of the state. (Some states have community property laws; others have equitable distribution.) The court ultimately decides what is fair, usually dividing the number of years of marriage by the number of years the employee has participated in the plan to determine how much of the 401(k) account is a marital asset. The participant and spouse may also negotiate any split of the 401(k) account acceptable to both.

A Qualified Domestic Relations Order (QDRO) must be filed by the spouse's legal representative. It requires the 401(k) administrator to divide the participant's account as dictated by the court. The spouse has all the usual rights of a plan participant for his or her share of the 401(k) assets, including the right to leave the money invested in the plan (unless the QDRO requires the money to be paid out immediately).

If an ex-spouse opts not to roll his or her share into an IRA, the money will be subject to income tax; but in a divorce, the IRS waives the 10% early withdrawal penalty that would normally be levied on any distribution made to a participant under age 59½. A divorce court can also order that part of the 401(k) balance go to the couple's children. By law, if the children roll the money into an IRA taxes will be due on it. The children, however, don't pay the taxes; *the participant does.* The 10% penalty is waived when payments are made to the children.

SMART PILL: Be aware that many QDROs are legally invalid since they do not conform to the provisions of the plan.

(For a more detailed discussion of QDROs, See"QDROs," pages 48-49.)

123 **Can my spouse empty my 401(k) account without my knowledge?**
A spouse shouldn't be able to touch a penny of a participant's retirement account unless the participant dies or the couple gets a divorce. But spouses are *not only legally entitled* to be designated beneficiaries of 401(k) accounts, the Internal Revenue Code *requires them to be the named beneficiary* in all qualified retirement plan accounts unless they've signed a consent waiver surrendering the right.

124 **Can I empty my 401(k) account without my spouse's knowledge?**
Maybe not. If your plan follows joint-and-survivor rules, spouses are legally entitled to receive a share of the 401(k) distribution in the form of lifetime annuity payments. In that case, your plan may require spousal approval of any loans or hardship withdrawals participants wish to take. The degree of protection extended to a non-participant spouse depends on specific plan provisions.

125 What happens to my 401(k) account if my company goes out of business?

Participant accounts are completely protected if your company goes out of business. The plan sponsor is required to deposit 401(k) contributions in a separate trust account (or in a contract with an insurance company) within a reasonable period after they have been deducted from participants' pay. As a separate legal entity, the trust continues. The plan's trustee(s) are responsible for managing the 401(k) money until all benefits have been paid to participants. Creditors of the company have no legal claim to 401(k) funds. *However, any contributions deducted from your pay that have not been deposited into the plan are at risk.*

126 What happens to my 401(k) account if my company is sold?

It depends on the benefit programs and policies of the acquiring entity.

If the acquiring company or individual owns other business units, all of which are covered by the same 401(k) plan, your business unit may be required to join that same plan. In that case, contributions after the sale may have to go into the new company's plan. There may be a coverage gap for several months as employees become eligible for the new plan. Their existing account balances will probably be transferred to the new plan.

Frequently the acquiring company prefers that each business unit maintain its own benefit program, in which case your existing plan would be retained with little or no change. If your plan features do not merge easily into the new plan, your plan will probably be maintained until these issues can be resolved. If, however, the other businesses owned by the acquiring company do not have a 401(k), it's entirely possible that your plan could be terminated.

In many cases, if participants continue in their old job, or in any other position with the acquiring company, they won't be entitled to a distribution even if, technically, they become the employee of a new entity. The IRS reasons that there has been no real "separation from service" entitling the plan to make a distribution.

127 Can the company use my 401(k) contributions to run its business?

Absolutely not. Plan sponsors are required to invest 401(k) contributions according to plan provisions and the law. It is illegal for companies to use the money for any other reason.

128 What rights do I have as a participant if I have a dispute with the company regarding my 401(k)?

By law, all 401(k) plans must establish a claims review procedure and all participants are entitled to receive a copy. When participants have a dispute, their first step is to file a written claim with the official plan administrator—the person or committee responsible for the day-to-day administration of the plan. The plan administrator is required to respond in a timely manner, explaining why benefits are being denied. If the participant remains dissatisfied, he or she has the right to request a review of the matter by the plan administrator. If the dispute is not resolved satisfactorily, the participant can seek the help of an attorney and/or the Department of Labor.

THE RESOURCE GUIDE IS A SERIES OF SPECIAL SECTIONS INTENDED TO ENHANCE THE EDUCATIONAL VALUE OF THIS BOOK AND EXTEND ITS USEFULNESS AS A REFERENCE TOOL AND RESOURCE.

➤ UNDERWRITER PROFILES

➤ ANNOTATED BIBLIOGRAPHY

➤ GLOSSARY OF INVESTMENT TERMS

➤ INDEX TO PART II:
THE MOST COMMONLY
ASKED 401(k) QUESTIONS

➤ SUBJECT INDEX

Access Research, Inc.

8 Griffin Rd., North, Windsor, CT 06095
Phone: 203-688-8821 • Fax: 203-688-2053

Key Contacts:
Robert G. Wuelfing, *President*
Gerald M. O'Connor, *Director of Research*
Jeffrey S. Close, *Director of Communications*

The Company:
Access Research, Inc. has an international reputation as
a premier provider of research, consulting and communications services to the employee benefits industry. A
recognized expert in the 401(k), 401(a), 408(k), 403(b)
and 457 markets, service providers, asset managers and
plan sponsors consider the firm an authority on the marketing and administration of 401(k) plans. Access has
helped many organizations enter the marketplace and
define their market strategies.

Access Research relies on its comprehensive market
database and extensive industry expertise to help
companies evaluate their current capabilities relative
to market needs, identify and evaluate strategic options,
and implement various marketing, plan design and
communications projects. Examples include product
development support, technology application evalua-
tions, and development of tactical marketing plans,
communication materials and sales support tools.

Access provides general communications strategy
and planning counsel, as well as design and writing services for employee and field communications.

Services:
- **Comprehensive Business Consulting**
  — Market Positioning Plans
  — Strategic Alliance Development
  — Distribution Planning

- **Strategic Research**
  — Customer Satisfaction Surveys
  — Market Awareness
  — Product Concept Development and Testing

- **Communications**
  — Public Relations and Employee Communications
  — Graphic Design
  — Multi-Media Marketing Campaigns

Aetna Investment Services, Inc.

Aetna Life Insurance and Annuity Company (ALIAC)
151 Farmington Avenue, RC5R
Hartford, Connecticut 06156

Key Contacts:
Laura R. Estes, *SVP ALIAC Pensions*   203-273-2850
Edward J. Lavelle, *SVP Sales/Marketing*   203-273-5866
                                          (Fax) 203-273-8193

Years in defined contribution/401(k) business: 13

**Total ALIAC assets under
management from all sources*:**   Over $18 Billion

Frequency of valuation: Daily

Services offered:
Although most often known as an insurer, Aetna Life
and Casualty Company and its affiliated companies is
one of the world's largest providers of financial services
to corporations, public and private institutions and individuals. ALIAC, a wholly owned subsidiary, manages
equity and fixed-income assets for retirement savings
plans (defined contribution and defined benefit); variable and fixed annuities; individual retirement accounts
and individual retirement annuities; life insurance policies and mutual funds. Through extensive separate
account and mutual fund products, ALIAC has the
resources and expertise to establish long-term customer
relationships. Aetna Investment Services, Inc. is the distributing broker/dealer for ALIAC's registered products.

Assets managed by client category*:

	ASSETS
Corporate pensions	over $5.0 Billion
Public/government	over $2.5 Billion
Endowments & foundations	over $ .4 Billion
Healthcare & education	over $6.0 Billion
Individual	over $4.0 Billion

*As of 12/31/94

Investment approaches:
ALIAC applies a long-term, below-market risk investment strategy for both equity and fixed-income portfolio
management. Fixed-income managers employ a disciplined, top-down approach based on duration, yield
curve, sector and security. For our broadly diversified
equity portfolios, securities selection is based on value,
growth and other quality factors related to fund investment objectives. To complement ALIAC funds, we also
offer a wide range of funds managed by highly respected
outside fund managers.

American United Life Insurance Company® (AUL)

P.O. Box 368, Indianapolis, Indiana 46206-0368

Key Contacts:
Brian Sweeney, *VP Pension Marketing*   317-263-1161

Year Founded: 1877

Pension Assets Under Management: $3.7 Billion

PRODUCT	NO. OF CASES	ASSETS
401	2,059	$1.2 Billion
403(b)	4,271	$1.6 Billion
457	358	$459.6 Million
408	949	$53.3 Million

(as of 12/31/94)

Special areas of expertise:
AUL offers a variety of asset class alternatives managed by industry experts such as Fidelity Investments® and Twentieth Century Investors® among others. The AUL Fixed Interest Account demonstrates AUL's financial strength and sound investment strategy.

Frequency of reporting results:
Quarterly performance updates through newsletter. Daily valuation and transfers available through toll-free number.

Service Approach:
A leader in retirement savings programs, AUL has offered companies a wide range of full-service products for more than 30 years. With more than 7,000 plans and 300,000 participants, AUL successfully combines quality service and cutting-edge products to maintain a client retention rate of more than 90%.

Defined Contribution Plan Expertise:
- 401(k)
- Profit-sharing
- IRA/SEP
- Deferred compensation agreements
- Money purchase
- TDA

Available services:
- Prototype or customized plans
- Assistance with required governmental filings and tests
- Quarterly employee reports
- State-of-the art recordkeeping services
- An integrated trustee services plan
- An in-depth communications program

CIGNA Retirement & Investment Services

350 Church Street, Hartford, CT 06103
Phone: 800-997-6633 • Fax 203-725-2052

Key Contacts:
Douglas E. Klinger, *Senior Vice President Marketing & Business Development*
Frederick C. Castellani, *Senior Vice President Sales & Services*

Assets Under Management:

Discretionary Assets	$59 Billion
Tax-Exempt Assets	$34 Billion
401(k) Assets	$17 Billion

Special Areas of Expertise:
CIGNA, with over 70 years of institutional investment management and retirement plan experience, is one of the nation's leading providers of retirement plan services. With 25 dedicated regional offices nationwide, CIGNA manages retirement assets for more than 5,000 organizations including public and private corporations, unions, associations and government entities. We offer a full range of bundled and unbundled services, a flexible, state-of-the-art relational database daily recordkeeping system and comprehensive investment options through our Multi-Manager Matrix of nationally recognized investment managers.

Investment Approach:
CIGNA Retirement & Investment Services offers single-source accessibility to a comprehensive array of top-performing investment products from CIGNA and other major mutual fund complexes and independent money managers. The foundation of our approach is our rigorous screening, selection and performance measurement process designed to provide the benefit of advance due diligence to plan sponsors. Our key objective is to provide access to consistently superior investment strategies across all major asset classes.

Retirement and investment products are provided by subsidiaries of CIGNA Corporation, including CIGNA Investments, Inc. and Connecticut General Life Insurance Company.

Fidelity Investments®

82 Devonshire Street, Boston, MA 02109

Key Contacts:
Fidelity Institutional Retirement Services Company
(A division of Fidelity Investments Institutional Service Company, Inc.)
Robert Reynolds, *President*   617-563-2888
Peter Smail, *Senior Vice President*   617-563-0335

Year Founded: 1946

Assets Under Management:

	No. of Clients*	Assets*
Total FMR:	8M *shareholders*	$2.75 Billion
Total Retirement Services Company:	5,500	$70 Billion

*as of 12/31/94

Special Areas of Expertise:
Fidelity Management & Research Company offers a range of mutual fund products to institutional and retail clients. Fidelity Management Trust Company provides separate account management and commingled pools to institutional investors through a range of investment disciplines.

Investment Approach:
For all our disciplines, our investment philosophy is consistent with Fidelity's 48-year history.

Fundamental Research:
We base decision-making on in-depth knowledge of companies and credits.

Adherence to Investment Disciplines:
A consistent, well thought-out investment discipline governs each portfolio's objectives, investment universe, buy and sell disciplines, desired characteristics and expected performance pattern.

Fully Invested Portfolios:
Fidelity does not engage in market timing.

Portfolio Managers Have Responsibility and Accountability:
Within their disciplines, portfolio managers have broad investment latitude and unlimited access to resources, and they are strictly accountable for performance.

Harris Investment Management, Inc.

190 South LaSalle Street, 4th Floor
P.O. Box 755, Chicago, Illinois 60690-0755
Telephone: 312-461-7699 • Fax: 312-765-8169

Key Contacts:
Carol H. Sullivan, *Senior Partner*
Marketing and Client Services   312-461-6567

Year Founded: 1909
an SEC registered firm since 1990

Total assets under management from all sources: $13.3 Billion

Special Areas of Expertise:
Harris Investment Management offers investment management and advisory services for the following asset classes:

Equity: Large Cap, Passive and Enhanced S&P 500 Index, Small Cap, International

Fixed Income : Active Bond, Intermediate, Active Cash, Structured, Municipals

Balanced: Stock/Bond, Multi-Asset, Convertibles

Frequency of Reporting Results: Monthly

Assets Managed by Client Category:

	No. of Clients	Assets Managed (in millions)
Employee Benefit	126	$9,019
Endowments/Foundations	67	696
Taft-Hartley Funds	18	854
Other Tax-Exempt	25	453
Taxable	37	1,122
Other	22	1,191

Investment Philosophy:
• Investments should be actively managed to accomplish specific objectives in light of each client's unique circumstances.
• Superior performance results from a disciplined investment process based on identifying and exploiting predictive factors.
• The application of analytics to an investment process significantly increases the consistency of its results.
• Experienced investment professionals are essential to each facet of the investment process.

Kemper Financial Services, Inc.
Kemper Distributors, Inc.
120 South La Salle Street, Chicago, IL 60603
Phone: 800-621-1148 • Fax: 312-499-5207

Key Contact Information:
Edward Miner, *Vice President*
Retirement Plan Marketing   800-621-1148

Year founded: 1948

Total assets under management from all sources:
                              $59 billion as of 12/31/94

Minimum account size: $1,000
(For plans set up on KemFlex the minimum account size is $25.00)

Special areas of expertise:
As one of the nation's largest money managers, KFS offers a variety of investment alternatives, including 21 open-end and 6 closed end mutual funds and money market funds, and provides investment management and advisory services. Kemper is an experienced qualified plan provider with more than $3.7 billion in retirement plan assets under management. Two powerful plan management tools which set us apart: KemFlex and the KemFlex Organizer. KemFlex provides accurate and timely reporting while the KemFlex Organizer quickly gathers, inputs and transmits plan data on-line to the KemFlex accounts.

Frequency of reporting results: Quarterly
(For plans set up on KemFlex reporting can be as frequent as monthly)

Assets managed by client category:
Defined contribution plans for profit organizations

Investment approaches:
KFS strives to provide high-quality asset management based on teamwork, a clearly defined investment style and thorough research. In both its equity and fixed-income mutual funds, KFS generally focuses on total return, as measured by income and capital gain.

LaSalle National Trust, N.A.
135 South LaSalle Street, Chicago, IL 60674-9910

Key Contacts:
Robert Hudon Jr., *Senior Vice President*   312-904-2497

The Company:
LaSalle National Trust is an affiliate of ABN AMRO, N.V., one of the largest banks in the world. While its main office is in The Netherlands, the bank operates in 66 countries around the world. In 1979, ABN AMRO acquired LaSalle National Bank, beginning a pattern of growth that has led to its becoming the largest foreign bank in the United States, with nearly $50 billion in assets. With global assets of more than $285 billion, it is one of the 20 largest banks in the world and it carries a double A credit rating.

Assets Under Management:
Worldwide $40 Billion
Includes several mutual funds in The Netherlands and Luxembourg.

Domestically $5 Billion
Includes the Rembrandt Funds® (a variety of 14 mutual funds), the second largest pooled GIC fund in the country, and separately managed equity and fixed-income accounts.

401(k) Services
We provide a comprehensive package of 401(k) services focusing on middle-market companies. Our services provide you with state-of-the-art recordkeeping which includes daily valuation capabilities, a flexible telephone voice response system and complete compliance and tax reporting. We offer mutual funds from a variety of fund families, including our proprietary funds (Rembrandt®), which allow plan sponsors flexibility in creating an investment menu for their participants. The real strength of our program lies in our customized and continuous communications program that is based on our commitment to helping you increase participation and make employees better investors.

MetLife

One Madison Ave., New York, NY 10010

Key Contacts:

Nicholas Latrenta, *Vice President*	212-578-3761
Gary Lineberry, *Vice President*	212-578-3181
Felix Schirripa, *Vice President*	212-578-6492

**Total tax-exempt assets under
management from all sources:** $77.1 Billion

**Wholly Owned Investment
Management Subsidiaries:**

State Street Research & Management Company actively manages equity and fixed-income assets for individual and institutional separate accounts and mutual funds. MetLife Investment Management Corporation (MIMCO) provides active fixed-income management of diversified, mortgage-backed, asset-backed, private placement, and duration-constrained portfolios for individual and commingled separate accounts. GFM International Investors, Ltd., London, specializes in active non-U.S equity and fixed-income management of separate account and mutual fund products.

Number of Clients (all sources):

Corporate Funds	1,323
Public Funds	118
Unions (Taft-Hartley)	89
Foundations & Endowments	8

Investment Approaches:

State Street Research draws upon specialized internal research and "bottom-up" equity analysis. A "top-down" fixed-income philosophy utilizes interest rate forecasting, yield curve analysis and duration constraints. MIMCO achieves incremental return to fixed-income portfolios through duration management, sector weighting, issue selection, yield curve analysis and interest rate anticipation, with emphasis on credit and quantitative research. GFM's active management strategy includes country allocation, currency weighting and issue selection. In the firm's core macroeconomic view, equity selections are based upon fundamental valuation methods, while fixed-income issues are selected through the variation of interest rate exposure, yield curve analysis and maturity structure.

NYL Benefit Services Company

A New York Life Company
One University Office Park, Waltham, MA 02254

New York Life Asset Management
51 Madison Avenue, New York, NY 10010

Key Contacts:

NYL Benefit Services Company:
Jim Wironen

Senior Vice President, Marketing	800-586-1413
Susette Deering, *Vice President, Marketing*	800-586-1413

New York Life Asset Management:

Linda Livornese, *Vice President*	212-576-7416

Year Founded:

NYL Benefit Services Company	1970
New York Life	1845

Assets Under Management:*

New York Life

Consolidated Assets	$68.9 Billion
Total Tax-Exempt Assets	21.5 Billion

*as of 12/31/94

Special Areas of Expertise:

NYL Benefit Services provides a full range of record-keeping and benefits consulting services. New York Life Asset Management offers a range of investment products from the conservative to the aggressive. A full spectrum of mutual funds is available through NYLIFE Distributors Inc., member NASD. Guaranteed products, including the Pooled Stable Value Account, as well as Separate Accounts, are offered by triple-A rated* New York Life Insurance Company.

* Independent services rate companies on a number of factors, including financial strength and performance and claims-paying ability. Several of the leading services gave New York Life their highest rating—Moody's Investors Service: Aaa, based on financial strength; Standard & Poor's and Duff & Phelps Corporation: AAA for claims-paying ability; and A.M. Best Company, Inc.: A++ (Superior) for financial stability.

Prudential Defined Contribution Services (Pru-DC)

30 Scranton Office Park, Moosic, PA 18507

Key Contact Information:

Robert E. Lee, *Vice President*
Marketing & Communications Group   717-341-6005

History:

Founded in 1875, The Prudential has been a manager of pension assets since 1928. In 1963, The Prudential began providing investment management, recordkeeping and educational communication services to defined contribution plans. In 1992, Pru-DC, an independent business unit, was established to provide full-service defined contribution administration to the mid-sized market.

Total Assets Under Management
From All Sources (The Prudential): $297 Billion*

Defined Contribution Assets: $30 Billion*
($8 billion full-service, $22 billion stable value investment only)
*Both figures as of 12/31/94

Reporting of Valuation: Daily

Minimum Account Size: $1 Million

Special Areas of Expertise:

Pru-DC is dedicated to providing institutional investment management, recordkeeping and investment education services. The diversity of investment choice available at Pru-DC—mutual funds, separate accounts and conservative stable-value options managed over the long-term—is attractive to any investor. We offer some of the industry's most experienced investment professionals, recognized for their specialized investment expertise. Our advanced recordkeeping system integrates image processing, a voice response system and daily valuation to ensure responsive, efficient service. We also provide a specialized team of professionals dedicated to implement new plans to ensure a smooth transition to Pru-DC. Award-winning investment education materials round out our services to give employees comprehensive, flexible and effective investment communications.

T. Rowe Price Associates, Inc.

100 East Pratt Street
Baltimore, MD 21202

Key Contacts:

T. Rowe Price Retirement Plan Services, Inc.
(A subsidiary of T. Rowe Price Associates, Inc.)

Charles E. Vieth, *President*   410-547-5763
John R. Rockwell, *SVP, Sales*   410-547-2077

Year Founded   1937

TRPA Assets Under Management: $58 Billion
(as of 12/31/94)

Special Areas of Expertise:

T. Rowe Price Associates offers a wide range of mutual funds and investment management services to institutional and retail clients. Retirement Plan Services is the subsidiary dedicated to meeting the needs of the defined contribution market. A pioneer in offering mutual funds as retirement options, T. Rowe Price provides investments, plan sponsor services, and participant services that can be tailored to meet a client's specific needs.

Investment Approach:

T. Rowe Price's investment approach is based on fundamental research and strict adherence to fund objectives. We seek consistent, strong, risk-adjusted performance.

Plan Sponsor Services:

T. Rowe Price provides plan sponsors with a complete array of recordkeeping and plan-related services. Clients benefit from more than a decade of experience in providing innovative solutions.

Participant Services:

T. Rowe Price has for years been at the forefront of investor education. We are committed to helping participants understand how to plan and invest to achieve a financially secure retirement.

ANNOTATED BIBLIOGRAPHY

RECOMMENDATIONS FROM THE AUTHOR AND INVESTORS PRESS

Not surprisingly, the explosion in 401(k) plans has also triggered an information explosion. These are a few of the most worthwhile information sources according to plan sponsors.

ORGANIZATIONS

50 Plus Pre-Retirement Services, an affiliate of The Reader's Digest Association, Inc., produces extensive retirement planning support materials, including a monthly magazine, brochures and videos. Call (212) 366-8852.

The Financial Literacy Center produces a series of colorful, easy-to-read and inexpensive brochures to help educate 401(k) participants, as well as *Loose Change*, a newsletter written under the direction of the Institute of Certified Financial Planners. Call (616) 343-0770 or (800) 334-4094.

The 401(k) Association, founded by Ted Benna, provides a hotline as well as information services for plan participants. These include its investment guide, *Planning for Tomorrow*, and *Legislative Update*, a quarterly newsletter. Call (215) 579-8830.

The Institute of Management & Administration (IOMA) is a leading independent publisher of information services for the defined contribution market. IOMA publishes 25 newsletters and reports of interest to plan sponsors. Call (212) 244-0360.

The Profit Sharing Council of America (PSCA), a non-profit association of 1,200 companies and their two million employees, provides help with plan design, administration, investment, compliance and communication. Besides envelope inserts and educational videos, PSCA publishes an "Annual Survey of Profit-Sharing and 401(k) Plans" and produces a variety of materials for plan administrators. (312) 441-8550.

Standard & Poor's Corp., an early independent source of 401(k) information, offers an Asset Allocation Service for plan participants, along with *Your Financial Future*, an investment newsletter. Contact Robert Meynecke at (212) 208-8967.

BOOKS, REPORTS AND VIDEOS

"**The Wealthy Barber,**" a highly acclaimed educational video, and its sequel, "**The Wealthy Barber Returns**," are based on the bestselling novel of the same title by Dave Chilton. Inspired by the TV series "Cheers," both book and videos use humor to educate employees about financial and retirement planning. The book, from Prima Publishing, Sacramento, CA, 1992, is available in bookstores. For bulk orders, call (800) 665-3913. For videos call (313) 876-8161.

The Fund Analyst provides low-cost, customized mutual fund portfolio reports for individuals. Clear and easy to navigate, these quarterly market value and performance reports have monthly updates. Call Tom Fischer at (800) 399-3008.

The 401(k) Provider Directory by David Huntley and Joseph Valleta (Towson, MD, 1995), provides detailed information on leading 401(k) vendors, including fees, investment options, administration, recordkeeping and communications. Worksheets help plan sponsors comparison shop. Call (800) 462-0628 or (410) 296-1086.

The 401(k) Plan Management Handbook: A Guide for Sponsors and Their Advisers by Jeffrey M. Miller (Chicago, IL: Probus Publishing Company, 1993). This first-rate, readable guide to establishing and overseeing 401(k) plans features helpful sections on investment policy, fiduciary responsibility under ERISA (with particular attention to regulatory grey areas), and the legal requirements of the Internal Revenue Code.

How ERISA Section 404(c) Affects You and Your Firm's Retirement Savings Plan by Luke D. Bailey, Esq. and Dale W. Schultz, PFP (Emeryville, CA: Schultz, 1993). A clear, concise 65-page guide to understanding 404(c) in the larger context of ERISA, including definitions and interpretations of fiduciary liability. Co-authors Schultz (an investment counselor) and Bailey (an ERISA attorney) specialize in defined contribution plans. Call Dale Schultz at (415) 291-3000.

Online Information

Reality Online, owned by Reuters, operates **Reuters's Money Network**, the largest online service dedicated to personal investing. Reality also publishes **WealthBuilder™**, one of the top-selling financial planning software programs for individuals. Call (800) 346-2024 or (610) 277-7600.

Also available online: **Morningstar publications**. This popular mutual fund rating service provides selected performance data on its universe of 5,500 funds to America Online subscribers as part of AOL's basic service. Call AOL at (800) 827-6364. Check other online offerings from **Prodigy**, (800) 776-3449, and **CompuServe,** (800) 848-8199.

Trade Publications

The following publications offer in-depth, ongoing coverage:

Pensions & Investments; Institutional Investor magazine (Julie Rohrer's monthly "Defined Contributions" column offers market intelligence on trends, new products and strategies); *Defined Contribution News*, Institutional Investor's bi-weekly newsletter, covers hirings and firings, legislation and regulation, and features plan profiles and sponsor forums; *Employee Benefit News* is a good source of industry news and trends and benefit management techniques. Also of note are: *Employee Benefit and Plan Review; Plan Sponsor Magazine; Corporate Finance*; and *CFO Magazine*.

The 401(k)/Defined Contribution Service Providers section of the *Money Market Directory* profiles leading 401(k) and defined contribution financial service providers with contact information and key personnel, assets under management, number of sponsor clients and plan participants, available services (including toll-free number support) and each firm's investment and service philosophy.

Suggestions from the Underwriters

Access Research, Inc. suggests two of their reports. Call Gerry O'Connor at (203) 688-8821:

"401(k) Participant Attitudes and Behavior," 1994. This survey of over 1,300 participants reveals their attitudes about investing, information sources they rely on, how they allocate contributions among investment options, and the events motivating them to change contribution amounts or asset allocation or to transfer funds.

"Defined Contribution MarketPlace Dynamics IV," 1995. A two-part study of current and projected trends on market needs and service satisfaction based on input from 1,500 defined contribution plan sponsors. A fourth edition of this study is scheduled for release in mid-1995.

Aetna suggests the following four articles:

"Partners for Profits in the 401(k) Market," by Caroline Alden, *LIMRA's MarketFacts*, March/April 1994, pp. 22-23. This article discusses various types of strategic alliances and how they are shaping the defined contribution marketplace; it appears in a publication of the Life Insurance Marketing and Research Association. Call LIMRA at (203) 688-3358.

"Understanding Advantages in New Retirement Plan Withdrawal Rules," by E. Thomas Foster, Jr., *Pension World*, April 1993, p. 28. This article covers the different rollover rules that apply to participants receiving plan distributions, as well as pitfalls participants should avoid when requesting payouts.

"Boosting Exec Pensions Within Existing Plans," by E. Thomas Foster, Jr., *Pensions & Investments*, February 20, 1995, p. 14, discusses how highly compensated employees can offset the loss of tax deductions caused by the $150,000 compensation cap.

"Consider More Than One Option in Putting Aside Money for Retirement," by E. Thomas Foster, Jr. and Susan J. Lewis, *Los Angeles Business Journal*, September 19, 1994, p. 43. Besides advocating a varied approach to retirement investing, the writers discuss how to avoid the negative consequences of withdrawing too much money or having an excess accumulation in a qualified plan at death.

CIGNA Retirement & Investment Services recommends:

"Let the Sponsor Beware," by Lynn Brenner, *CFO Magazine*, October 1994, p. 57. This article points out that many 401(k) providers are focused on market share rather than cost-effective services. The writer contends that 401(k) providers need technological and service excellence, not just recordkeeping capability.

Delaware Management Company, Inc. offers the following four internally produced articles. Fax request to Bonnie Rockhill at (215) 988-1681:

"Mutual Fund Mathematics" by Julia R. Vander Els, Vice President–Institutional Retirement Services. This educational series addresses mutual fund concepts for defined contribution plan participants, such as total return, fund distributions and dollar-cost-averaging.

"Everyone is a Long-Term Investor Until the Market Goes Down!" by Paul E. Suckow, Chief Investment Officer–Fixed Income. Focusing on the dramatic losses in the bond market during 1994, this article analyzes the sources of fixed-income returns and how market conditions affect results.

"Derivative: The Bond Market's New Dirty Word?", also by Paul E. Suckow, provides an overview of derivative instruments, including basic terminology, product types and risk factors.

"When is a Mutual Fund the Wrong Answer for Your Plan?" by Minette van Noppen, Vice President/Managing Director–Institutional Retirement Services. This report contrasts the mutual fund vehicle in today's defined contribution plan with the more traditional investment structure of an individually managed portfolio—an evaluation of fees, performance and operational requirements.

Harris Investment Management, Inc. recommends:

Basic Points, by Donald G.M. Coxe, President and Chief Investment Officer, Harris Investment Management, Inc. (HIM). This monthly report offers a fresh look at the global forces moving capital markets, along with an investment outlook and asset allocation guide. Fax request for a free subscription to Linda Kemp at (312) 461-7096.

Kemper Financial Services, Inc. and Kemper Distributors, Inc. suggest:

For Your Benefit, their quarterly newsletter on personal finance and retirement planning for plan participants, is available by calling (800) 621-1048; request KEF-1 and KQP-4H.

MetLife suggests:

"The Ins and Outs (and Ups and Downs) of Book Value Wrappers," by Alec Stais, CFA, ASA, Vice President, MetLife Investment Management Corporation, explains book value wrappers commonly associated with synthetic GICs. To request a copy, call Mark Foley at (212) 578-6872.

GLOSSARY OF INVESTMENT TERMS

Asset allocation: The process of dividing your money between different types of assets—such as stocks, bonds, cash, and real estate—in a combination intended to generate the overall return you need, while minimizing your overall risk. The underlying idea is that if you own assets that behave differently, you'll always have one or two investments that are doing okay. The history of financial markets shows that owning both stocks and bonds is less risky than owning only stocks or only bonds.

Average maturity: A bond matures when it stops paying interest and repays investors' principal. The average maturity of a mutual fund's bond portfolio is the average length of time it takes those bonds to mature. A fund with a longer average maturity pays a higher yield. But if the prevailing interest rate rises, your principal will lose more value than it would in a fund with a shorter average maturity.

Basis point: A unit of measurement that makes it easy to measure dollar amounts smaller than one percent. One percentage point equals 100 basis points. In other words, an investment that yields 3.5% pays 500 basis points more than one yielding only 3%.

Bear market: A bear market is one that loses value for an extended period of time, typically a year or more.

Big-cap stocks: The stocks of companies whose market value—the total number of shares outstanding multiplied by their price—is more than $10 billion. Big-cap companies are well-established corporations with a long track record of steady earnings growth and reliable dividend payments.

Blue-chip stocks: Shares in the nation's biggest and most consistently profitable companies. There's no official list of blue-chip companies because they keep changing.

Bond: An IOU issued by a corporation or by a government. The bond issuer is borrowing money from you and other investors. (The U.S. government is the nation's biggest borrower.) Most bonds pay interest at regular intervals until they mature, at which point investors get their principal back. Alternatively, some bonds are sold at a discount to their face value—$800 for a $1,000 bond, for example. The investor gets $1,000 when the bond matures, receiving interest and principal repayment in a lump sum.

Bond rating: A way of measuring the bond issuer's ability to make good on its IOUs. The major bond rating agencies are Standard & Poor's Corp. and Moody's Inc.

Buy-and-hold: A long-term investing strategy. Buy-and-hold investors maintain their holdings, ignoring short-term market fluctuations. The opposite of buy-and-hold is market timing: trying to anticipate market trends in order to sell investments before prices fall, and buy again before prices rise.

Bull market: A market that gains value for an extended period, often several years. Even in a bull market, however, prices fluctuate from day to day.

Capital appreciation: The growth of your principal. If you invest $100 in a stock mutual fund and its value increases to $120, that $20 increase is called capital appreciation.

Capital gain: When you sell an investment for more than you paid, your profit is called a capital gain. If you sell for less than you paid, you have a capital loss.

Cash investment: A very short-term loan to a borrower with a very high credit rating. Examples of cash investments are bank certificates of deposit (CDs), Treasury Bills (T-Bills) and money market funds. A cash investment typically offers investors great principal stability, but little long-term growth.

Commercial paper: Very short-term IOUs of highly rated corporate borrowers. The maturity of these loans ranges from overnight to 90 days. Money market funds are a big buyer of commercial paper.

Commodities: Raw materials like wheat, gold, silver, oil, pork bellies, oranges, cocoa. Commodities are an extremely volatile investment—their value can soar or plummet overnight.

Common stock: An ownership share in a corporation.

Compounding: Compounding happens when you earn interest not just on your original investment, but also on the interest it has already earned. If you earn 10% a year on an investment for four years, and let your interest compound, for example, instead of earning 40% over these four years, you actually earn 46.4%. The longer you stay invested and automatically reinvest your earnings, the more dramatically compounding can increase the value of your investment.

Correction: A relatively short-lived drop in market prices. (It's called a correction because professionals consider it a return to appropriate values.)

Credit rating: See Bond rating.

Debt: On Wall Street, "debt" is a synonym for investments in which you lend your money for a specific term and rate of interest—i.e., bonds.

Default: The bond issuer's failure to pay the interest or principal that has come due on his bonds.

Distribution: A mutual fund's payment to shareholders of the profits, interest, or dividends it has earned on its investments. Outside a 401(k) account, distributions would be taxable income unless they represented interest the mutual fund earned on tax-exempt investments. But inside a 401(k) account, your distributions are tax-deferred and automatically reinvested, giving you the great benefit of compounding. (See Compounding, above.)

Diversification: A fancy way of saying don't put all your eggs in one basket. You diversify by spreading your money among several different investments; that way, you won't be too badly hurt if any one of them performs poorly.

Dividends: Income paid by your investments. Both stocks and bonds can pay dividends. Mutual funds pass the dividends they earn on their investments to their shareholders. In a 401(k) account, these dividends aren't paid to you in cash, but are automatically reinvested to buy more shares for you.

Dollar cost averaging: An investment technique in which you invest a fixed amount at regular intervals—$100 at the beginning of every month, for example. With dollar cost averaging, you automatically buy more shares when the price is low and fewer shares when the price is high. As a result, your average cost is less than the average share price.

Dow Jones Industrial Average: The stock price average of 30 blue-chip stocks that represent about 15% to 20% of the market value of the stocks traded on the New York Stock Exchange.

Equity: Equity is an ownership interest. On Wall Street, "equity" is often used as a synonym for stock—i.e., an equity investor is a stockholder. By contrast, a debt investment is one in which you lend money. You invest in a debt instrument when you buy a bond.

Expense ratio: The percentage of a mutual fund's net assets that is used to pay its expenses. The higher a fund's expense ratio, the bigger the bite being taken out of your return to pay those expenses.

Fixed-income: A synonym for bonds, which promise a fixed rate of interest until they mature. Bond mutual funds are called fixed-income funds, but the name is misleading because in a bond mutual fund your income fluctuates. Your principal value also fluctuates (both in individual bonds and in bond funds) as the prevailing interest rate changes. When the interest rate rises, existing bonds lose value because they now pay a lower-than-prevailing rate. When the interest rate drops, the value of existing bonds goes up because they now pay a higher-than-prevailing rate.

Global fund: A mutual fund that invests in stocks and bonds all over the world, including the United States. By contrast, an international fund invests all over the world except in the United States.

Growth investment: An investment whose main objective is to grow your principal rather than to generate income. A house, a gold coin, and a stock mutual fund are all growth investments. You hope to make money in a growth investment by eventually selling it for a lot more than you paid for it.

Guaranteed Investment Contract (GIC): A contract between an insurance company and an investor that promises to pay a fixed rate of interest and to return principal after a specified term, usually one to five years. "Guaranteed" doesn't mean you can't lose money. A GIC is guaranteed only by the issuing insurer, not by the government or by your 401(k) plan.

Income investment: An investment whose main objective is to generate income in the form of interest or dividend payments, rather than to grow your principal. A bond fund, for example, is an income investment.

Individual Retirement Account (IRA): A personal tax-deferred retirement account that can hold any type of investment. You can own IRAs at many different financial services companies, but your total annual IRA contribution cannot exceed $2,000. Whether or not your IRA contribution is tax-deductible depends on your income and on whether you participate in a pension plan or 401(k) plan.

Index: A statistical model that judges how well an investment is performing. The benchmark most often used for stock market performance is the Standard & Poor's 500 Index, which measures the average performance of 500 widely held common stocks. Over periods of 15 years or longer, the stock market, as measured by the S&P 500 Index, historically has earned an average 10% annual return.

Index fund: A mutual fund that buys the stocks or bonds that make up a widely used market index. The goal of an index fund is to mirror market performance.

International fund: See Global fund.

Lump sum distribution: A single payment representing the entire amount due to you from your 401(k) plan.

Management fee: The fee a mutual fund pays to its investment advisers. This fee is expressed as a percentage of fund assets, and is paid by the mutual fund's shareholders.

Market timing: An investment strategy based on predicting market trends. A market timer may buy or sell investments based on a conviction that interest rates will rise or fall, for example. The goal of market timing is to anticipate trends, buying before the market goes up and selling before the market goes down.

Maturity: A bond's maturity is the length of time it takes to repay investors' principal. (See Average maturity, above.)

Money market fund: A mutual fund that invests in the very short-term IOUs of the government and highly rated corporations. Money market funds pay a fluctuating interest rate, but maintain a fixed $1 per share value. (See Net asset value.)

Mutual fund: An investment company that pools the money of many individual investors and uses it to buy stocks, bonds, money market instruments and other assets.

Net Asset Value per share (NAV): The value of a single share in a mutual fund, which is determined daily by dividing the total assets of the fund, minus its liabilities, by the total number of shares outstanding.

Principal: The amount you originally invested.

Pre-payment risk: A risk assumed by anyone who invests in mortgage-backed bonds. The risk is that the prevailing interest rate will fall, causing homeowners to pay off their existing mortgages. When that happens, investors in mortgage-backed bonds get their principal back much sooner than they expected, and must reinvest it at the lower prevailing interest rate.

Rollover: Moving money from a 401(k) plan into another tax-deferred retirement account, like an Individual Retirement Account, so that you avoid any tax liability.

Share: A unit of ownership in a corporation or a mutual fund.

Small-cap stocks: The stocks of companies whose market values—total number of shares outstanding multiplied by their price—are less than $500 million. Small-cap companies grow faster than big-cap companies and typically use any profits for expansion rather than for paying dividends. But they're also more volatile than big cap companies and fail more often.

Standard & Poor's 500 Index: See Index, above.

Total return: The total that you're earning on an investment. Total return is the dividends and interest you get, plus any change in the value of your principal, or original investment. If your mutual fund share price increased from $23 to $25, and you also received a 20 cent per share dividend, your total return was $2.20—a little over 9%.

Treasuries: The IOUs of the U.S. government. The Federal government borrows money by selling Treasury bills, which range in maturity from 90 days to one year; Treasury Notes, whose maturity ranges from one to ten years; and Treasury Bonds, whose maturity ranges from ten years to 30 years.

Treasuries are considered to have no risk of default. But like all bonds, they are vulnerable to interest rate risk. (See above.)

Turnover ratio: The percentage of a mutual fund's holdings that was replaced during a one-year period. A fund's turnover ratio tells you how aggressively the portfolio manager buys and sells investments. You can find this information in the prospectus.

Value: In Wall Street slang, a value investor is an investor who looks for stocks selling for less than they're really worth. By contrast, a growth investor looks for stocks of companies whose earnings are growing rapidly.

Yield: The annualized rate at which your investment earns income.

NOTE: Yield is not the same as total return. It's possible to earn a good yield on an investment, but lose money anyway because of a drop in principal value. A $1,000 bond that pays 10% will continue paying 10% after the prevailing interest rate rises to 11%—but the bond will be worth less than $1,000.

INDEX TO THE MOST OFTEN ASKED 401(k) QUESTIONS

CHAPTER FOUR: UNDERSTANDING 401(k) PLAN INVESTMENTS

CHAPTER FIVE: INVESTMENT TERMINOLOGY

SUBJECT INDEX

➤ **A Wing and A Prayer:** *Defined Contribution Plans and the Pursuit of 24 Karat Golden Years*

Book II – 1994 Investment Management Series

In this ground-breaking book, distinguished industry professionals from Apple Computer, Halliburton and Eastman Kodak examine the fundamental—and specific—challenges facing defined contribution plan sponsors as they struggle to meet their fiduciary responsibilities.

(96 Pages, hard cover — $45 per copy; limited supply available)

➤ **Building Your Nest Egg With Your 401(k)**

by Lynn Brenner

Written specifically for 401(k) plan participants, **Nest Egg** explains why it is so important for them to save as much as they can—as early as they can. In easy to understand, layman's language **Nest Egg** features the answers to more than 100 of the most commonly asked employee questions and explains how to create an investment strategy for retirement that's truly easy to implement.

(160 pages, soft cover, fully illustrated — $18 per copy; published June 1995)

➤ **Helping Employees Achieve Retirement Security**
An Investors Press Guide for 401(k) Administrators

by R. Theodore Benna

(144 pages, hard cover — $45 per copy)

Please allow two weeks for delivery of all books. Specify the quantity and titles you are ordering. Prices include shipping and handling. Please mail payment to:

Investors Press, Inc.
P.O. Box 329
Washington Depot, CT 06794

Investors Press is pleased to invite each of its readers to reserve a complimentary copy of the second book in the 1995 DC Plan Administrator Series.

Publication: November 1995

To reserve your complimentary copy of the second Guide, mail or fax comments on **Helping Employees Achieve Retirement Security**, to us along with your name, title and mailing address.

Complimentary copies will be provided by Investors Press and the distinguished group of co-sponsoring providers of the second Guide.

Investors Press
Fax: 203-868-0715

To receive information about Underwriter participation, please contact:

P.O. Box 329, Washington Depot, CT 06794
Telephone: 203-868-9411 • Fax: 203-868-9733